RESPECTFUL
REHABILITATION

RESPECTFUL REHABILITATION

ANSWERS TO YOUR QUESTIONS ABOUT OLD BUILDINGS

**Technical Preservation Services
National Park Service
U.S. Department of the Interior**

Drawings by David J. Baker

The Preservation Press

The Preservation Press
National Trust for Historic Preservation
1785 Massachusetts Avenue, N.W.
Washington, D.C. 20036

The National Trust for Historic Preservation is the only private, nonprofit organization chartered by Congress to encourage public participation in the preservation of sites, buildings and objects significant in American history and culture. Support is provided by membership dues, endowment funds, contributions and grants from federal agencies, including the U.S. Department of the Interior, under provisions of the National Historic Preservation Act of 1966.

Many of the questions and answers presented in this book appeared originally in *Historic Preservation*, the magazine of the National Trust for Historic Preservation. The magazine is a benefit of membership in the National Trust. For information about membership, write to the Trust at the above address.

Library of Congress Cataloging in Publication Data

Respectful rehabilitation.

    Bibliography: (p. 173).
    Includes index.
    1. Historic buildings—United States—Conservation and restoration. 2. Historic buildings—United States—Remodeling for other use. 3. Historic buildings—United States—Maintenance and repair. I. National Trust for Historic Preservation in the United States. II. United States. National Park Service. Technical Preservation Services Division.

NA106.R43 1982   720'.28'80973   82-15018
ISBN 0-89133-103-4

Designed by Tom Engeman
Composed in Benguiat by VIP Systems, Inc., Alexandria, Va.
Printed by Collins Lithographing and Printing Company, Baltimore, Md.

Cover: Amariah T. Prouty House (c. 1853), Kalamazoo, Mich. Photograph by Balthazar Korab.

CONTENTS

FOREWORD

Today nearly a million buildings are listed in the National Register of Historic Places, either individually or as part of registered historic districts. These—and countless other old buildings—require not only continuing maintenance and preservation but also the rehabilitation needed to accommodate new uses dictated by changing times. While many owners, architects and contractors are familiar with modern construction technologies and products, relatively few have had extensive experience dealing with historic buildings. In addition, many of the materials suitable for new construction are not appropriate for rehabilitating historic buildings. Thus, there is a real need for sound advice on how to carry out rehabilitation work that respects the historic and architectural character of our built environment.

To help meet this need, Technical Preservation Services (TPS) of the National Park Service has published and continues to develop a wide range of technical information about methods and techniques for maintaining, preserving and rehabilitating historic buildings. While some of this literature has been highly technical in nature, most of the publications have been intended for wide distribution. The Preservation Briefs series, for example, covers subjects from cleaning masonry to repairing historic wooden windows; more than 500,000 have been distributed since 1976.

Many of the same questions are asked repeatedly of TPS by historic property owners. Thus, when the National Trust for Historic Preservation approached us to respond to readers' questions and prepare a new question-and-answer column for its magazine, *Historic Preservation,* we viewed the column as a unique opportunity to provide advice to a wide audience.

Our answers to the questions selected for inclusion here reflect a rehabilitation rather than a restoration philosophy and are based on the Secretary of the Interior's Standards for Rehabilitation and the accompanying interpretive guidelines (see p.159). As defined in the standards, "rehabilitation" means "the process of returning a property to a state of utility through repair or alteration that makes possible an efficient contemporary use while preserving those portions and features of the building that are significant to its historical, architectural and cultural values." The standards are the criteria by which rehabilitation projects are evaluated to determine whether the character of historic buildings has been preserved for purposes of federal rehabilitation tax benefits; they also have been adopted by a number of historic district and planning commissions across the country.

The questions that follow may be ones you have asked or have wanted to ask or should be asking about how to rehabilitate an old or historic building with respect. Whether your problem is paint or plaster, ceilings or floors, heating or air conditioning—or all of these—we hope that this information will help you plan and successfully accomplish your rehabilitation project.

Lee H. Nelson, AIA, Chief
Technical Preservation Services
National Park Service
U.S. Department of the Interior

ACKNOWLEDGMENTS

This book was developed by the staffs of Technical Preservation Services of the National Park Service and the Preservation Press of the National Trust for Historic Preservation, under the direction of Kay D. Weeks, technical writer-editor, TPS, and Diane Maddex, editor, Preservation Press books. Key TPS staff contributors included Anne E. Grimmer, architectural historian, who reviewed the technical content of the answers; Sharon C. Park, AIA, architectural historian, who assisted with preparation of technical illustrations; and Michael J. Auer, who helped conduct illustration research and compiled bibliographic materials. Sara K. Blumenthal, real property program specialist with TPS, served as contract and scheduling liaison with the Trust. The work of Technical Preservation Services was supervised by Lee H. Nelson, AIA, division chief; Gary L. Hume, deputy division chief; and H. Ward Jandl, Preservation Projects Branch chief. Baird M. Smith, AIA, former chief, Preservation Technology Branch, initiated the project before leaving TPS.

Answers to the questions were prepared by the following present and former technical staff of TPS: Gary R. Arabak, Michael J. Auer, Sara K. Blumenthal, James A. Caufield, Charles E. Fisher III, Alex Griego, Anne E. Grimmer, Gary L. Hume, H. Ward Jandl, Brenda S. Johnson, Frederec E. Kleyle, David W. Look, AIA, William G. MacRostie, Robert P. Meden, AIA, ASID, John H. Myers, Sharon C. Park, AIA, Baird M. Smith, AIA, Christopher A. Sowick, James C.A. Thompson, deTeel Patterson Tiller, Jean E. Travers and Kay D. Weeks. Additional questions were answered by Phillip M. Spiess II, formerly of the National Trust.

The book was edited by Gretchen Smith, associate editor, Preservation Press.

I am interested in buying an old house and renovating it, but I am concerned about one thing: If the house is located in a historic district, will I be able to make all the changes that I want?

You should first contact the mayor's office or local planning agency to determine whether the house is located in a historic district. Keep in mind that the boundaries of such districts are subject to change. A house that is not now included in a historic district might later fall within the boundaries of an enlarged district, or the neighborhood itself might later be declared a new historic district.

If the house is located in an existing district, obtain a copy of the establishing ordinance. Most historic district ordinances create a commission charged with reviewing changes to existing buildings and designs for new construction. Historic district commissions usually have the authority to prohibit demolition of buildings and alteration of exteriors, as well as to order a stay of demolition or alteration. The purpose of historic district ordinances is not to prevent property owners from making changes to their buildings but to avoid inappropriate alterations that affect buildings and their neighborhoods. Commissions will generally work with property owners to reach a compromise on design changes that will not alter the character of the district.

You also should find out whether the property is covered by protective easements, covenants or deed restrictions. A former owner might have attached a restriction to the deed limiting the right of future owners to alter the architectural character of the building. In many cases the right to enforce such restrictions has been assigned in perpetuity to a third party, such as a local preservation organization or the state historic preservation office.

I have purchased a 100-year-old building, which I cannot afford to rehabilitate until next year. Although the building is deteriorating, the routine inspection before the sale revealed no structural problems. I am worried, though, about leaving the building vacant and in need of repair. Is my worry justified?

You are right to be concerned. A provisional building and site protection plan (often referred to as "mothballing") should be developed immediately to protect your building. Measures should be taken to secure the building from fire and vandalism. These should include installing a fire and burglar alarm system connected directly to the police and fire departments; notifying neighbors and the police of where you can be reached and your intent to rehabilitate the building; inspecting the electrical system to ensure that no fire hazards exist; preventing all means of entry by animals and unauthorized persons; and removing all trash and debris from the yard and inside the building.

Vacant buildings can be seriously damaged by moisture because they are often unheated during the winter, and leaks from the roof or basement can go undetected for some time. Measures should be taken to prevent moisture buildup. Roofs and drainage systems should function properly. Heat should be provided during the winter, if possible. If not, some outside ventilation should be provided in each room and especially in the attic, basement and crawl spaces. When implementing these measures, such as when installing alarm systems and securing windows and doors, take care that as little as possible of the historic building material is damaged. After these measures have been taken, the building should be inspected periodically so that any problems can be corrected or stabilized as soon as possible.

Buildings were meant to be occupied, not left vacant; thus, some deterioration or damage is inevitable even though you take all these precautions. This plan may entail immediate expenses that you did not foresee when you made your purchase; however, unless these measures are implemented, you may not have a building to rehabilitate next year.

We recently purchased a turn-of-the-century house in a town that seems to have old houses of nearly every age, shape and description. How can we find out what style our house is and learn more about how to identify other old local buildings?

The key to identifying the style of your house is to understand its architectural history and evolution, not just prevalent American architectural styles. A number of books can help you identify major styles (see Reading About Rehabilitation), but what you see in these reference books is not always what you will see on your street or elsewhere. Most buildings reflect combinations of styles or adaptations of local building traditions and materials; because many early structures were built by unsophisticated but competent builders removed from the mainstream of architectural fashion, it is difficult to find ''pure'' examples of textbook styles except for the most expensive and sophisticated buildings of the period. Some buildings simply defy stylistic labels: They may have been designed in a period when architectural fashions were changing, or they may have resulted from purposeful efforts to create styles different from their neighbors. Moreover, although stylistic terms are most useful in attempting to describe visual features of buildings, some frequently used terms—such as ''colonial'' or ''Victorian''—actually refer to historical periods and tell little about specific appearances.

Alterations and additions over the years also may change the character of a building and thus further confound efforts to categorize its style. In planning a rehabilitation, it is important to respect later alterations because these may have significance in their own right. You should not try to create a house that never existed, so avoid the arbitrary removal of later features in attempting to restore your house to a particular style.

In addition to consulting architectural reference books, you should consult your local historical society and state historic preservation office. Here you may find documents that can assist you in researching your property, such as old photographs, drawings and records pertaining to your house and its neighborhood.

GEORGIAN

ITALIANTE

GREEK REVIVAL

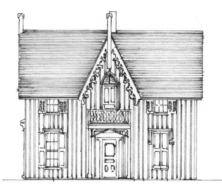

GOTHIC REVIVAL

QUEEN ANNE

BUNGALOW

Are photographs an acceptable method of documenting a structure's existing condition before rehabilitating it? If so, please explain how they can best be used.

Your concern for adequate documentation before starting your project is commendable. Photographs are an excellent means of recording existing conditions and are highly suited for conveying detailed information that is both time-consuming and expensive to prepare using other methods (for example, measured drawings).

For photographs to be helpful, several factors should be noted: (1) Photographs should be black and white because color reproduction is often inaccurate, can be misleading and can fade; (2) depending on the subject, photographs should be at least 8 by 10 inches to maximize clarity and detail; (3) photographs should be liberally annotated so that what is pictured is also adequately described; and (4) a scaled measure such as a yardstick, ruler or other uniform scaled device should always be included in the photographs to indicate the dimensions of the features included. The subject should be photographed straight on to minimize distortion caused by perspective. A large-format view camera with distortion correction capability will produce ideal results, but sometimes the expense of this type of equipment prohibits its use.

I am considering donating a facade easement on my 1890s commercial building in a historic district. Will I qualify for any federal tax advantages?

Under the Tax Treatment Extension Act of 1980, owners of historic buildings may qualify for substantial income and estate tax deductions by donating conservation easements on their buildings. Unlike the tax credits for rehabilitation, the deduction for an easement donation applies to structures that are used solely as private residences as well as income-producing buildings.

A conservation easement is a legal document that regulates the use of or changes to a certified historic structure. To qualify for the tax benefits, you should first contact your local or state easement-holding organization to see whether it would be interested in accepting your easement and to obtain further advice on completing necessary forms. Then contact your state historic preservation office to have your property certified as contributing to the historic district. Your property also must be appraised by a qualified real estate appraiser to determine its value before and after the donation of the easement. The value is determined by appraising the unrestricted fair market value of the property, taking into account its full development potential allowable under current zoning regulations. The projected market value of the property with the restrictions imposed by the easement is then calculated. The difference between the two appraisals is the value of the easement and is the amount that owners can take as a charitable contribution deduction. Because conservation easements run in perpetuity and are a binding encumbrance on your property deed, you will need to have an attorney prepare the legal papers.

I am considering rehabilitating an old building I own and have been told that in doing so I might qualify for certain tax advantages. Is this information correct? If so, what are the benefits?

You did not indicate what kind of building you own or how old it is, but it is possible that important new tax provisions may apply to you. The Economic Recovery Tax Act of 1981 contains significant preservation tax incentives. Among other provisions, this law allows a 25 percent investment tax credit for rehabilitation of historic income-producing buildings—commercial, industrial and residential. The credit is deducted from the amount of taxes owed, in contrast to a deduction that merely reduces a taxpayer's income subject to taxation. The investment tax credit can be combined with a 15-year cost recovery period for the adjusted basis of the historic building.

Note that the building undergoing rehabilitation must be a commercial, industrial or rental residential building subject to depreciation as defined by the Internal Revenue Code. Property owners who live in certified historic structures and use the rest of the building for commercial or residential purposes can claim a 25 percent investment tax credit, on a prorated basis, for rehabilitating the income-producing portion of the building. A property owner may not use the 25 percent investment tax credit if the historic building is used solely as a private residence.

Before the tax benefits accrue to an owner, however, the building must be certified as historic by the Secretary of the Interior. This means that it must be listed individually in the National Register of Historic Places or located in a registered historic district and certified by the Secretary of the Interior as being of historical significance to the district. The Secretary of the Interior must also certify that the rehabilitation work undertaken is consistent with the historic character of the property or the district in which the property is located.

If the old building you own is not historic, you may still qualify for a lower tax credit: 20 percent for work on buildings 40 years or older, and 15 percent for buildings 30–39 years old. These credits are limited to nonresidential industrial and commercial buildings used for income-producing purposes. The law further provides that owners or lessees of historic structures cannot deduct expenditures or losses resulting from demolition beginning after June 30, 1976, and before January 1, 1984.

Owners of historic houses should also be aware that certain states and localities provide tax incentives for maintaining and rehabilitating designated historic structures. Owners should contact their state historic preservation office for more information on all types of rehabilitation tax benefits.

I have always wanted to own and rehabilitate an old house, but I never have been able to afford to buy one. However, I have a chance to purchase a Victorian house that will otherwise be demolished to make way for a new civic center. I am considering having the house moved across town, but I have heard some negative reports about this approach to preserving a historic building. Should I move the house or not?

Moving a historic building is not recommended as a preservation treatment—unless it is the only way to save the building from demolition. When a historic building is moved from its original location it loses some of the historical significance associated with its setting, to say nothing of the inevitable loss of historic fabric, such as plaster, and the possible damage to the structure itself. However, because this house is slated for demolition, moving it is apparently the only option. If you decide to move the house, you should try to move it intact, if possible, rather than dismantle it. Complete dismantling results in considerable loss of original fabric, and the building ends up as essentially a reconstruction rather than a restoration. Selection of a new site for the building is also important; the terrain and location (urban or rural) should be similar to the original setting.

I recently bought a large Greek Revival house dating from the 1840s and plan to convert it into an office for my medical practice. The most convenient place for a parking lot, from the perspective of easy access for patients, is in front of the house; however, placing it here would mean removing a tree, plantings and part of a walkway. There is room for a parking lot behind the house, but placing it there would mean cutting a driveway alongside the house. Any suggestions?

In planning an adaptive use project, it usually is possible to make compromises that are sensitive both to the client and to the building and its environment. From the preservationist's point of view, distinguishing landscape features that have traditionally linked buildings to their environment—such as gardens, street lights, benches and walkways—should be retained. New construction should be unobtrusive and should alter landscape features as little as possible.

Placing your parking lot at the front of the house will dramatically alter the relationship between the building and its environment. Of the two options, putting the lot at the rear of the building is preferable. That way, the driveway can be screened from view by a hedge or fence or by a combination of hedge and fence. The back entrance of the house near the new parking lot would provide easy access for patients.

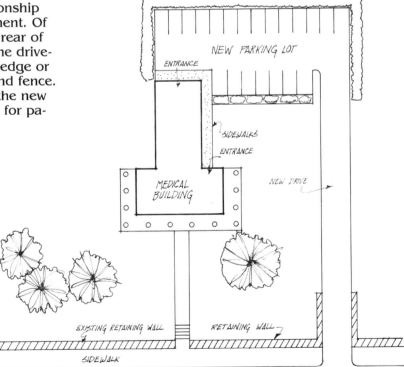

In recent months I have heard more and more about acid rain and the increasing national concern about its effect on the natural environment. What is acid rain? Does it have an adverse effect on historic buildings as well?

Acid rain results from the combustion of large quantities of fossil fuels such as coal and oil, which discharge huge amounts of sulfur and nitrogen oxides into the atmosphere. Through a complex series of chemical reactions, these pollutants are converted into acids, which then return to earth in rain and snow. Although the full extent of possible adverse effects of acid rain on land areas is not yet known, its effects on bodies of water is well documented. In fact, hundreds of lakes in North America and Scandinavia have become so acidic that they can no longer support fish life.

From these data, it is clear that acid rain also is probably hastening the destruction of stone buildings and monuments throughout the world. For example, the Parthenon in Athens, Greece, because of the city's high level of air pollution, has shown more rapid decay in this century than it has in its previous 2,500 years. Such deterioration has been difficult to measure accurately, but international efforts have begun in an attempt to quantify the effects of acid rain on stone buildings. In the United States, the Environmental Protection Agency, working with the National Park Service and the U.S. General Services Administration, in 1980 installed instruments on the Bowling Green Custom House (1901–07) in New York City in a first attempt to monitor and analyze acid rain run-off on this historic granite and limestone building. Data gained from the scientific analysis will be used to help devise methods and techniques for protecting historic stone buildings from premature deterioration due to acid rain.

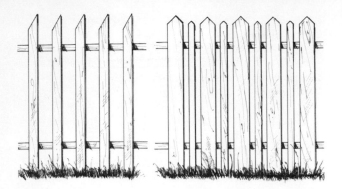

My neighbor and I would like to replace the rusting chain link fence between our 19th-century houses. What kind of fence might be appropriate for rural Georgia?

A fence in wide use in the South during the 19th century was a picket fence with pickets slanting on one side only, the other remaining straight.

If you have a garden or a planted border along your property line, you might want to build a lath-and-picket fence. This kind of fence resembles a typical picket fence, except that the pickets are five inches apart. Similarly pointed strips of lath are then nailed between the pickets. A runner as wide as the pickets is then attached at the bottom. This type of fence is authentic and also helps protect against rabbits and other pests.

A year ago I inherited my grandparents' farm, which is located in a rural western Massachusetts community blessed with both historic houses and lovely country-side. My wife and I have no plans to work the farm ourselves. We would prefer to sell the property to someone willing to continue operating the farm, but so far the only offer has been from a developer. Is there anything else we can do? We love the community and would like to help retain its special flavor.

Preservationists in growing numbers share your concern not merely for buildings but for neighborhoods and communities—the context within which buildings assume their significance. The burgeoning interest in community preservation has proceeded side by side with increasing interest in land conservation in general. One result has been the Rural Project of the National Trust. Another has been an explosive growth in the number of land trusts, many of which seek to help people in your situation. Land trusts can assist sellers in locating sensitive buyers; some trusts buy properties for resale with preservation restrictions attached.

For more information on land trusts, contact the Land Trust Exchange (3 Joy Street, Boston, Mass. 02108), publisher of the *National Directory of Local Land Conservation Organizations.*

Our local preservation group is interested in establishing a sign ordinance for our neighborhood historic district. Can you advise us?

As a general rule, any sign ordinance should have as its goal compatibility between the signs and the architectural style of the buildings with which they are associated. Each sign should be clear, concise and readable. It should not overpower or detract from the overall streetscape but, instead, become a part of it. For help in writing an ordinance, contact your local historic district commission, planning agency, state historic preservation office or the National Trust for Historic Preservation.

Our street in a local historic district is virtually intact. The historic district ordinance offers some protection against development and unsightly alterations, but we have no assurance that the future climate here will be sympathetic to preservation. The ordinance could be changed, or officials could overlook violations. What can my neighbors and I do to ensure the future preservation of our street?

You should explore the possibility of donating easements on your properties to a preservation organization. An easement is a right or interest held by one party in the property of another. The terms and duration of easements vary considerably, but preservation easements generally prohibit a property owner from making alterations to the exterior without the permission of the easement holder, and they usually are granted "in perpetuity." Because easements are legally enforceable, the easement-holding organization can take action to prevent violations.

Granting an easement on a historic property can also produce financial benefits for the donor. Reductions in federal income, estate and gift taxes and, in some places, state and local taxes as well may result from the donation of an easement to a qualified organization. The process of donating an easement can be complex. No one should embark upon it without first seeking competent legal and financial advice.

A number of national organizations will accept historic preservation easements. For more information, contact your state historic preservation office, local preservation organization and the National Trust for Historic Preservation. See also the *Directory of Historic Preservation Easement Organizations*.

In the garden of my Dutch Colonial stone house in New Jersey is an exceptionally large, spreading red oak tree. Local oral tradition maintains that the tree and an adjacent grove of red oaks marked the site of Indian encampments during pre—Revolutionary War days. Is there any way that I can determine whether the tree is old enough to give credibility to this legend? Also, could an archeological investigation prove or disprove this bit of oral history?

To determine the age of your red oak, you should contact a nearby university with a botany program to see whether someone on the staff could examine your tree and determine its approximate age; agricultural and mechanical schools are often able to provide such services. It may be possible to determine the age of the oak through dendrochronology (dating by comparative study of growth rings). If the grove of oaks adjacent to the tree has stumps or dead trees, cut a ring from one of the stumps or dead trees and have it analyzed; the age indicated by the ring might indicate the approximate age of the oak.

An archeological investigation could produce artifacts—for example, pottery sherds or evidence of hunting and gathering—that will help determine whether the site was occupied by Indians and, if so, the approximate dates of occupation. Your state historic preservation office can provide information about the possibility of undertaking such a project. A less expensive way to learn almost as much about your site is to research deeds, wills and journals of early travelers.

Our organization is involved in the rehabilitation and restoration of a late 19th-century mansion and grounds that are interpreted historically and are open to the public. Included in the 78-acre grounds are some original Italian garden architecture and sculpture—marble urns, fountains and a pergola—that need only minor repairs. Our problem is the handling of the planting beds themselves. At present, they are in fairly shabby condition, consisting only of a few indigenous flowers and shrubs. The architect wants to remove these plantings and create a more typical, formal Italian garden to ensure an authentic look for interpretive purposes. Unfortunately, all we have to document our restoration are three photographs from the early 1920s, and they show purely local plant types that are unrelated to Italian garden architecture. Can you give us any suggestions about how to approach the plantings?

Your garden restoration can be undertaken in three ways: (1) The unrelated plantings could be removed and replaced with authentic plantings, but this course of action must be based on an original planting scheme or plant list; (2) your photographs could be used to re-create the garden from the 1920s period or (3) the garden could be expanded using local plant materials and maintained more or less as is.

Creating a conjectural Italian garden that fits in with the garden architecture and sculpture is a tempting idea, but it lacks historical authenticity and will create a false impression for the public. The best solution would be to use the 1920s photographs as a basis for restoration—if they show enough of the gardens to be meaningful—and install an interpretive sign explaining that the current plant materials were probably not part of the formally planned Italian garden and are mostly of local origin.

On the north side of the apse of our brick church is a mosslike fungus covering the wall from the ground to approximately the height of the water table. This part of the church has no rain gutter. Could the lack of drainage be causing this growth? How can it be removed without damaging or staining the stonework?

From your brief description of the problem, it seems possible that you have a roof drainage problem or a site drainage problem (or perhaps both). The fungal growth is probably being caused by rainwater cascading off the roof and hitting the water table. If an unobtrusive gutter can be placed on the apse without changing the appearance of the cornice or wall, it should be installed. In addition, your problem may be aggravated by water standing at the base of the wall, causing further dampness in the wall through capillary action and splashing rainwater. After the gutter has been installed, it may be necessary to grade the earth around the base of the building to ensure that water drains away from the building. Once the problem has been corrected, the fungal growth can be removed with a solution of 1 quart household bleach to 1 gallon of water; scrub the affected area with the solution, using a medium-soft bristle brush. The wall should be thoroughly rinsed after scrubbing.

I recently purchased an 1850 brick Gothic Revival cottage. The plantings are overgrown, and some apparently old bushes are located close to the building's foundations. Cracks are beginning to appear in the brickwork, and I am afraid that the shrubbery may be the culprit. Should all the vegetation be removed?

Yes. However, if it is feasible and the cost is not prohibitive, you may wish to save the bushes and move them a reasonable distance from the foundation walls to prevent further damage. If you decide to remove the vegetation completely, it would be a good idea to cut down the bushes and vines; to prevent further damage to the building material, wait until the roots have dried out and have begun to decompose before removing them from the ground or the brick wall. You should then arrange to have the cracks in the brickwork repaired by a skilled mason who is sensitive to the needs of a historic masonry building—that is, one who will use a soft mortar that will not damage the old bricks.

I recently restored my house to its original Victorian style. Now I would like to restore the lawn. How would a typical midwestern Victorian lawn have looked?

If you have restored your house, presumably you have some sort of pictorial documentation that might assist you with the lawn. However, you may not be able to distinguish details. Also, you may not have as much land as the property originally encompassed, or the land may have drastically changed.

Victorian lawns usually were cut only four or five times during the growing season. The lawn texture was rather coarse and rough because of the type of seed used (often chaff from a haymow floor). The lawn mower came into common use in the 1860s; before then, lawns were grazed by sheep or cut with a scythe. To achieve a scythed look, try using a sickle bar mower after the grass has almost come to seed. You may be pleased to know that only wealthy Victorians weeded their lawns.

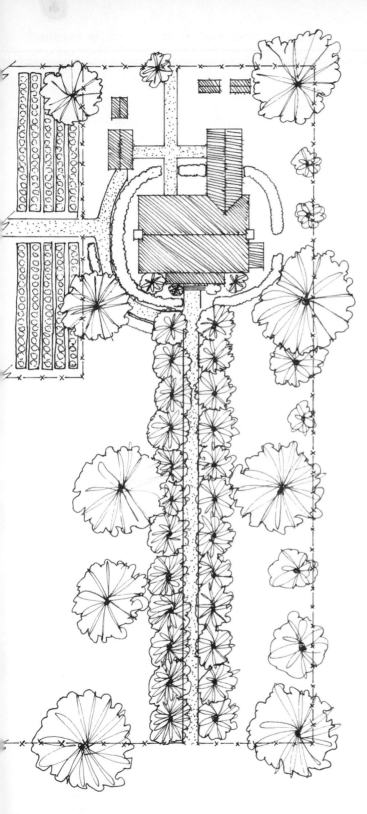

I would like to re-create the landscaping that surrounded my late 18th-century Georgian house. Unfortunately, I do not have a clue as to its original layout. Can you give me some general guidance?

In planning your landscape restoration, you should follow several important steps: (1) survey existing conditions, (2) research the original owners and their use of the property and (3) investigate the site thoroughly. The resulting information should provide you with adequate documentation for a comprehensive restoration plan with an appropriate selection of plant materials.

A survey of current conditions should produce a detailed account of all the existing features of your property. It is important to perform the survey before you remove or alter any of the existing features. Research into the original owners and their use will most likely provide information concerning their attitude toward the landscaping and possible types and locations of plant materials. During the period in which your house was built, the colonies had begun to prosper, and this prosperity allowed personal land to be used at least partially for decorative planting and landscape features.

A detailed site investigation should be undertaken both from the ground level and from an elevated vantage point. Small-scale aerial photography is also extremely useful for this type of investigation. From a distance you may be able to determine areas of garden plots, pathways and depressions over the foundations of early outbuildings that ground-level observation cannot provide. Archeological investigation can clarify the details of many features, such as pathway materials, specific plants and the exact location of outbuildings.

As with inappropriate changes or alterations to historic buildings, try to avoid period landscaping errors. Remember that foundation plantings, decorative shrubbery and many of today's favorite plants were not introduced or had not been popularized until the 19th century or later.

We have a severe drainage problem on the rear of our slab-on-grade 1940s house. Surface water drains toward the house and, together with rainwater runoff from the roof, has caused the earth under the slab to erode. We are on the downside of a hill, so regrading would be difficult. What should we do?

Being on the downside of a hill does not preclude regrading. However, if the land has swales or hills and valleys, regrading may not effectively rechannel the water around the house; in this case, you may have to build a small retaining wall. You should also consider attaching flexible drainage tubes to the end of the rear downspouts to carry roof runoff away from the back of the house.

REGRADE

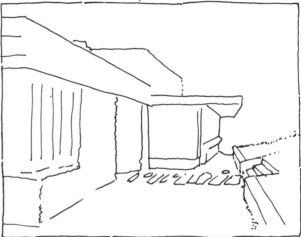

RETAINING WALL

BEFORE

My 18th-century farmhouse has old termite damage in several of the 4-by-8-inch wood joists in the basement. The house has been treated for termites and recently passed inspection, but the affected joists have been structurally weakened from past termite activity. Should I replace or simply reinforce the wood joists?

It is generally recommended that, if possible, the original materials of historic buildings be repaired rather than replaced. Because the historic wood joists are no longer actively infested, they can be reinforced with modern joists (new wood) on either side. If, on the other hand, you had a dry rot problem (in which the wood is attacked by a fungus), you would have to cut out the affected wood to halt the process of deterioration.

Generally speaking, whenever structural systems need repair, it is a good idea to consult an architect or engineer. In this case the architect or engineer could calculate the size of the new joists and determine how much bearing there should be at the support walls.

During the last 10 years, the number of buses passing in front of our 1892 house in Atlanta has increased from zero to 21 per hour. In addition, the buses are disruptive to the point of waking us at night, startling guests and rattling dishes and windows. Although the city transit department assures us that this vibration will not damage our house, I would like to know about any studies regarding damage to historic buildings caused by heavy traffic vibration.

The British seem to have done the most research in this area, yet none of their reports gives much specific information about the degree of damage to historic buildings caused by heavy traffic vibrations. Of course, heavy vibration can cause varying degrees of damage, and opinions differ as to what constitutes "damage."

If, however, you begin to notice severe cracks in the plaster that appear to be getting larger, you might want to contact a structural engineer to monitor the cracks with stress gauges. Various building materials and types of buildings are affected differently; for example, a detached, single-family house built of wood will probably suffer less structural damage than a more immobile masonry row house.

Perhaps the transit department is defining the problem differently from you and your family, who are constantly assaulted by the vibrations and the resultant noise. To make your point to the city, you will probably have to hire a seismic engineer or a professional structural engineer who specializes in analyzing the effects of traffic vibrations on buildings, preferably older or historic buildings.

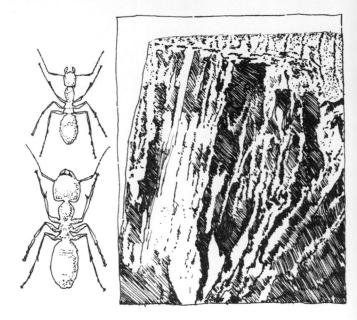

I have noticed large (about ½ inch long) black ants on my enclosed breakfast porch. Spraying with commercial ant sprays has not helped get rid of them. Could these ants be damaging my wooden porch? How can I get rid of them?

From the description of your unwanted guests, they are probably carpenter ants, and, yes, they can indeed do damage in a relatively short time. You should inspect the outside and the crawl space of the porch to determine whether any of the wood is moist, particularly around gutters and downspouts and under window sills. Carpenter ants build their colony nest by burrowing in moist wood but do not actually feed on the wood. Chances are that they are nesting in and possibly destroying some of the framing members of your porch and then coming onto the enclosed porch itself in search of food. The only sure way to get rid of the ants is to locate the nest, break up the colony and replace all moist (and probably damaged) wood. Using strong pesticides will not solve the problem because the ants will simply return and build a new nest.

Some of the row houses in my predominantly 19th-century residential neighborhood are decorated with metal stars. These stars are usually on the long side of the houses at the end of the row. Are these stars purely ornamental, or do they serve some practical purpose?

Cast-iron anchors, sometimes fashioned in the shape of stars, rosettes or S's, provide the only exterior evidence that a wrought-iron tie rod has been inserted through a building to prevent brick walls from buckling or separating further from interior walls. The rods, which are made of wrought iron because of its ability to take tension, were bolted to cross beams or to a parallel masonry wall. Occasionally tie rods were included in the original construction as a precautionary measure, but generally they were added later when an outer brick wall began to lean.

I have a decorative cast-iron stoop that has gradually sunk down on one side, and some of the iron is cracking. I want to save this nice feature of my house. Do you have any suggestions about how to go about it?

The major problem at this point is not the cast iron itself. The iron cracked because of differential settlement—one side of the stairs sank into the ground and the weight of the stoop was redistributed, causing forces too great for the cast iron to resist. Such settlement can be caused by the upward and outward growth of a tree adjacent to a stoop or the downward settlement of a dead tree stump as it decays. Whatever the cause of the buckling, no amount of patching or repair work on the cast iron will be effective until the structural problem is corrected. The stoop itself should be disassembled and a new concrete foundation poured. Then the stoop can be reassembled using any salvageable portion of the original stair. Any fractured sections can be repaired by welding on reinforcing pieces; missing elements can be recast at a local foundry.

I have recently moved to New Orleans and have purchased a 1920s brick house, which seems to be afflicted with something called "rising damp." Exactly what is rising damp, and what can be done to eliminate it?

Rising damp is the suction of groundwater into the base of brick and stone walls through capillary action. Moisture is drawn up into the somewhat porous walls and released at the interior and exterior surfaces, where a horizontal stain or tidemark is left. The moisture often carries with it salts (in solution), leaving efflorescence, which can cause deterioration of masonry, plaster, wood and paint. Although rising damp is a problem common in many old masonry structures, it is difficult to solve completely.

Rising damp often results from excess groundwater, so make sure rainwater does not collect at the base of a wall. There are several ways to ensure good drainage. One of the easiest solutions is to slope the grade away from the building. A second option, which is more difficult but often necessary, is to install drain tiles (often called French drains) around the structure. Although drain tiles will not completely eliminate the rising damp, they can minimize the problem and enable the walls to dry out. A third approach, more complicated but effective, is to construct a damp-proof course. Traditionally, damp proofing has been done by cutting out the mortar joints or course of brickwork at a level just above the ground and inserting a damp-proof course of slate or other impervious material. This process has largely been superseded by a simpler process of inserting rigid damp-proof material (bituminized fabric, polyethylene sheeting or lead sheets) into a narrow slot cut into the mortar joint. This system can be used on walls that are regularly coursed and stable. If the mortar has severely deteriorated, the wall may be too unstable for the joint to be cut out without dislodging masonry units above. For walls more than 8 inches thick, it may be necessary to work from both sides, one side at a time.

Another possibility may be to provide a chemical damp-proof course by injecting a waterproofing liquid through holes drilled into the brickwork in a continuous horizontal line around the building. When the liquid cures, it forms a continuous barrier to reduce capillary action. This method has recently been introduced into the United States from Europe.

The success of these treatments depends on specific conditions. You should attempt to correct the problem only after a qualified preservation architect or engineer has thoroughly investigated the house.

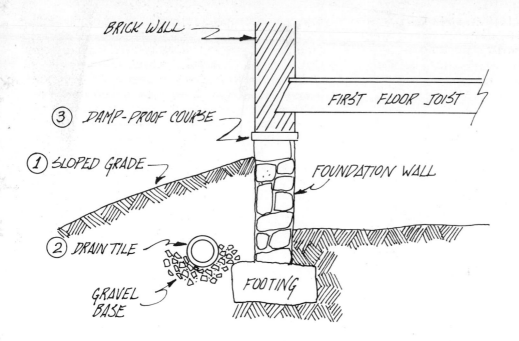

BRICK WALL

FIRST FLOOR JOIST

③ DAMP-PROOF COURSE

① SLOPED GRADE

FOUNDATION WALL

② DRAIN TILE

GRAVEL BASE

FOOTING

Our historic brick house is covered with ivy. Is it harmful to the brick?

There are more than 400 varieties of ivy and other climbing vines. These generally attach themselves to brick with small, hairlike tendrils, which contain small amounts of organic acids that have little effect on hard brick but are detrimental to soft brick. Ivy rarely sends roots into mortar joints, so the joints may not be seriously affected.

When ivy grows on a brick building, there is little to worry about, provided that the vines do not penetrate the wall through cracks in the brick or open mortar joints. If the brick and mortar have already begun to deteriorate, the growth of the ivy vines will hasten disintegration of the wall; in time, the ivy can widen cracks and even move bricks. The vines also hide deterioration and hinder inspection of cornices, gutters and downspouts.

Although the ivy leaves shield the brick from driving rain, they also shade the walls and reduce evaporation of moisture from inside the brick. If the walls have a moisture problem, such as rising damp or leaking gutters, the ivy may be contributing to the problem by slowing down evaporation. Moisture is usually more of a problem with soft, handmade brick, which is common in pre-1830 buildings.

Therefore, if your brick building is in good condition, the ivy may not cause harm; if not, it will probably hasten deterioration. Ivy should be regularly inspected and trimmed back from doors, windows, gutters and chimneys.

Several years ago I purchased a brick farmhouse in Pennsylvania built soon after the Civil War. Over the years, water running through the leaking roof has washed away much of the mortar on several sides of the house. Now that I have finally finished repairing the roof and replacing gutters on the house, I am ready to repoint the areas where the mortar has leached out. What should I know about repointing before I plunge in?

Historic brick buildings, particularly those built before 1900, were constructed with a soft, high-lime mortar generally consisting of sand and lime; sometimes, depending on the area of the country and the period, pigment or crushed shells were also added.

Mortar for repointing should be softer (in terms of compressive strength) than the bricks and no harder than the old mortar. Mortar that is stronger or harder than the bricks will not give and will cause any stresses within the building to be relieved through the bricks, possibly resulting in cracking and spalling of the bricks. Repointing mortar for most historic brick buildings should ideally be composed only of lime and sand; one part lime to two parts sand is a useful starting point. ASTM (American Society for Testing and Materials) C-150 Type I white portland cement may be substituted for up to 20 percent of the lime to achieve workability or plasticity without adversely affecting the most desirable qualities of lime mortar.

The size and profile of mortar joints are vital to the overall character of a masonry building. Thus, all joints must be carefully cut out by hand to a depth of one inch, and neatly repointed and tooled by hand. To reproduce the neat lines of the original joints so that the correct proportion of mortar to brick is retained, clean any excess mortar from the brick; if the repointing has been done skillfully, however, there should be no excess.

The most important thing to remember in repointing is that replacing mortar or repointing periodically is much easier and less damaging to the building than replacing damaged bricks.

	NORMAL	HOT (BRICKS EXPAND)	COLD (BRICKS CONTRACT)

FLEXIBLE MORTAR
(LIME)

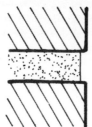 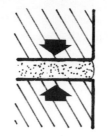 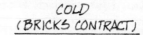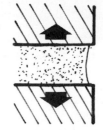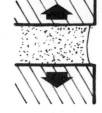

MORTAR COMPRESSES   MORTAR FLEXES

INFLEXIBLE MORTAR
(CEMENT)

 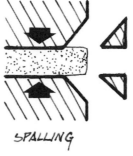 

SPALLING   CRACKS OPEN UP

The unpainted bricks on my 1887 Richardsonian Romanesque building have recently developed a spotty and unattractive white haze. What causes this haze, and how can I remove it?

The white haze on your brick building is efflorescence, the visible effect of salts within the mortar or masonry units coming to the surface and recrystallizing as moisture evaporates.

The presence of such salts is usually an indication of excess moisture in the wall, which is often caused by rain penetrating open mortar joints or cracked masonry units, by water leaking through roofs or downspouts, or by some other building defect. Efflorescence also can be caused by rising damp or excess moisture introduced during cleaning or repointing.

If the efflorescence is caused by physical defects in construction, it will continue, inevitably resulting in permanent damage to the masonry. Efflorescence caused by cleaning or repointing is not usually as harmful. In either case, you should eliminate the source of the moisture—for example, fix the roof—and then remove the efflorescence by brushing with natural-bristle (not wire) brushes. You may have to repeat this step several times, because additional salts may remain in the wall and continue to come to the surface.

The plaster on the inside of my brick walls often seems damp. Should I seal the exterior walls with a clear masonry waterproof coating?

No. Masonry sealers can cause serious damage by trapping moisture in the walls. Applying a sealer to brick with a moisture problem is like wrapping the building in a plastic bag. The moisture will be trapped, and the bricks will eventually spall because of freeze-thaw action or entrapped salt crystallization.

You should first determine where and how the moisture is getting into the walls. Look for leaking gutters, missing caulking and flashing around windows and doors, missing mortar between the bricks, hairline cracks in the masonry and improperly ventilated interior spaces, such as kitchens, baths and laundry rooms. Once the problems have been identified and repaired, the plaster on your walls should dry out.

SANDBLASTED
BRICK

UNTOUCHED
BRICK

Ten years ago, we sandblasted our 1891 building, and now the brick seems to be deteriorating. What can be done to prevent further damage?

Old brick, essentially a soft, baked product, is highly susceptible to increased deterioration when its outer skin is removed through abrasive cleaning techniques. The problem can be minimized by painting the brick or by treating it with a clear sealer. Painting is preferable because sealers tend to leave a glossy look and, more important, reduce the migration of moisture, allowing subflorescence—that is, salt crystallization—which causes spalling, or deterioration, of the brick. If the brick has been so badly damaged that spalling has already begun, it may be necessary to cover the walls with stucco or even replace the bricks.

What is the best way to remove tar from smooth pressed brick?

If the stains are limited to a few small areas, a poultice made of inert filler and an organic solvent can be used. Common solvents include acetone, benzene, xylene, naptha and mineral spirits. Apply the poultice about 1/4 inch thick. The dry powder or paste can be scraped off or brushed off with a natural-bristle brush. The application can be repeated if necessary. The cleaned area should be rinsed thoroughly with a detergent or water to remove any chemical residue. Because most organic solvents are highly flammable and sometimes toxic, extreme care is necessary.

Our 1887 church, which was moved and given a brick-veneer exterior surface in 1904, was severely damaged in a recent fire. The congregation is interested in rebuilding the church within the brick-veneer walls, if possible. Have the bricks been damaged as a result of the fire, and will they deteriorate, be more porous or spall in the near future?

Under most circumstances, bricks used as a veneer, rather than as structural support for a building, would not be affected by a fire, unless it were of an unusually high temperature. If, during the fire, the difference between the temperature on the inside face of the brick and the temperature on the exterior face was extreme, the brick would undergo thermal shock, resulting in cracking or splitting. This condition, however, should be readily observable during an inspection of the building.

Reusing the brick may pose an aesthetic problem: If the bricks have been badly stained by fire and soot or broken or chipped by falling structural members, the bricks may have to be replaced.

Another serious consideration in reusing the brick-veneer walls is that although the flames may not have affected the brick, they could have caused the mortar to carbonize. If this has happened, the mortar will have lost its structural properties, and the wall may be unstable and unsafe. You should have samples of the mortar chemically analyzed to determine its properties since the fire.

FORM-STONE

ORIGINAL BRICK

Can form-stone be removed from our brick row house?

Yes. The process is not too difficult, but it can be dangerous and should be done by an experienced contractor. Form-stone (often known by the trade name Permastone) was popular in the 1950s and 1960s. It was installed on expanded metal lath that was anchored into the brick or mortar joints, about 16 inches on center both vertically and horizontally. Anchors were sometimes spaced closer together around windows and doors and along eaves and corners. Sometimes the brick was given a coating of tar or bituminous waterproofing to create a vapor barrier that is difficult to remove. The lath was given a base coat of cement stucco, and then cookie-cutter-like molds filled with colored stucco were applied to the wet base coat.

Form-stone is very heavy and must be removed in sections. A masonry saw can be used to cut it into 4-foot-square sections. Starting under the eaves or wherever anchorage has been lost (usually noticeable because the form-stone is bulging from the brick), pry out the form-stone and peel it back to expose the anchors. An oxyacetylene blowtorch usually is used to cut the anchors. Anchors around openings and along edges tend to be the more difficult areas to remove. One house owner cut all the anchors around the windows; then, much to his surprise, the whole form-stone facade fell, just missing a car.

Before you begin, ask the contractor to remove a test patch to check the condition of the brick underneath. Damaged brick will need to be repaired. If anchors were driven into the mortar joints, they will need repointing. If the anchors were driven into the bricks, the damage could be severe, and many bricks may have to be patched or replaced. Projecting stringcourses and lintels were often chiseled off to allow the form-stone to be installed closer to the facade without bulges. If this is the case, you may decide to leave on the form-stone and learn to like it—you could paint it, stucco over it or plant ivy over it. Companies that install form-stone can repair your test-patch area if you decide not to remove the form-stone.

The slate window lintels on my 1880 commercial building, which is brick with stone trim, have deteriorated and are delaminating badly. Can you suggest a suitable technique for repairing them?

It is possible that the slate lintels can be saved and repaired with epoxy. Remove the deteriorating lintels from the facade and glue together the delaminating layers using an epoxy resin as an adhesive. Then reattach the repaired lintels to the facade in the window openings with either fiber glass or stainless steel reinforcing bars or rods. After reinstalling the lintels, fill in any spaces between the slate lintel and the brick wall with mortar using traditional repointing techniques.

The use of epoxy for stone repair is still quite experimental and thus may not be completely successful. However, it is probably worth trying if there is no other way of saving the slate.

Is there a preferred method for removing dirt from a historic limestone building?

No. Several cleaning methods, including water washing, steam cleaning and chemical cleaning, can be used on old or historic limestone. Each has advantages as well as disadvantages.

The gentlest method is probably water washing, a technique that includes prolonged spraying, aided by hand scrubbing with natural-bristle brushes, followed by a moderate-pressure (200–600 pounds per square inch) rinse. However, some limestones may be stained by impurities in the stone as a result of extensive water soaking, may dry unevenly and, because of their higher solubility, may even dissolve slightly.

The primary advantage of steam is its ability to clean ornately carved areas. But it is usually more expensive and often slower than water washing.

Chemical cleaners must be of an alkaline type, because limestone is extremely sensitive to acid. Alkaline cleaners consist of a detergent and some type of alkali, usually ammonia or potassium hydroxide. (Do not use sodium hydroxide on old or historic masonry because efflorescence and subflorescence are likely to result.) Rinsing is a two-part process: Give the masonry a slightly acid wash (possibly with acetic acid) and then a water wash to remove all the chemicals.

Vandals used felt-tip markers on a stone wall that surrounds my property. How can I remove the graffiti?

The stains can be removed with a poultice. A poultice is necessary to increase the amount of time the solvent is in contact with the stain and also to avoid the possibility of the stain's spreading or going deeper into the masonry. Prepare a poultice using a methylene chloride-based paint remover as a solvent; use talc, chalk or clay as a thickening agent. Apply the paste about ¼ inch thick. As the paste dries, it will draw the stain out of the masonry. When the poultice is dry, brush or scrape it off. Then rinse the masonry thoroughly with water. More than one application may be required.

I recently purchased an abandoned 100-year-old adobe church that I plan to restore. Some sections of the walls are in need of repair. Should I go to the expense of casting new "traditional" adobe brick, or is it appropriate to replace these sections with the new "stabilized" adobe brick selling throughout the Southwest?

Stabilized adobe (adobe brick that has been mixed with cement, asphalt or bituminous materials to make it water resistant) has been a boon to the new adobe construction industry in the Southwest. For this purpose its usefulness is unrivaled.

However, using stabilized adobe in this case is not advisable because of the peculiar characteristics of adobe. Adobe is, in the truest sense, organic—it is made from clay, sand, straw and grass, and is one of the oldest and most common building materials known. It is also inherently dynamic, like the soil from which it is made, and expands and contracts in proportion to its moisture content. Even in the arid Southwest there is substantial water from humidity, rainfall and high water tables. Adobe walls can expand and contract several inches in just a matter of days. Such flexibility is a normal characteristic of the historic material but not of stabilized adobe.

For this reason stabilized adobe will prove incompatible with the fabric of the old wall. The old wall will expand and contract within the normal cycle of the material; the stabilized adobe will not. In effect, part of the wall will be moving and part will not. The resulting tension and twisting will produce cracks or bulges in the wall. In some serious cases, the wall could collapse.

The concrete steps of our 1920s bungalow are showing signs of deterioration—some light scaling and hairline cracks. What should we do to restore the steps to their original condition?

An evaluation of the damage is essential in choosing the appropriate repair techniques for concrete. From your description, your problems do not sound serious. Chlorides from salts used to melt winter ice may well be the source of the deterioration; the use of salt on your steps should be avoided. However, damage may be due also to poor design or construction.

If the condition of the steps indicates only a loss of surface mortar but no exposure of coarse aggregate, the deteriorated areas should be cleaned of all loose materials and flushed with water. It generally is good practice to chip the edges of the deteriorated areas to make a better bonding surface. Many cracks, especially hairline cracks, do not require repair. Use a concrete patching material with a bonding agent to fill in the damaged areas; this material is available from most building supply or hardware stores. If color is important, a test patch should be undertaken; if a close match is not possible, you may wish to consider painting the steps for a uniform appearance.

Is it possible to remove heavy rust stains from my white marble front steps?

Removing rust stains from light-colored marble can be difficult, if not impossible, without damaging the stone, which is soft and porous.

Before cleaning, make certain that the source of the rust has been removed. You may have some luck using household bleach diluted with water or a commercially prepared rust remover. A solution of 1 pound of oxalic acid to 1 gallon of water with a small amount of ammonium bifluoride may also be effective on some of the lighter stains.

Because bleach probably will not remove rust that has soaked into the pores of the stone, also try a poultice; when left on the surface to dry, it will help pull the stain out of the stone. One such poultice consists of sodium or ammonium citrate, glycerine and warm water (in a proportion of 1:7:5) mixed with enough whiting (chalk) or talc to make a paste. Apply thickly over stained areas. It may be necessary to leave the mixture on overnight or longer, in which case you should cover the poultice with plastic to keep it from drying out too rapidly. Mixtures with acid solutions can etch sensitive materials such as marble if they are too strong or are left on for too long.

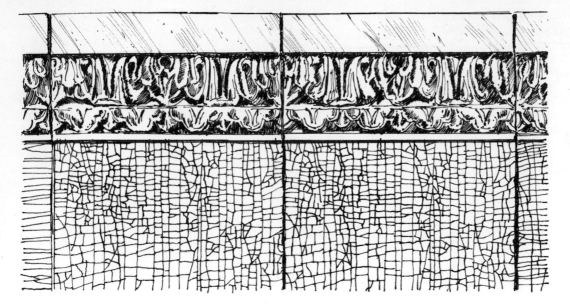

The glazed terra cotta on my Beaux-Arts bank building has crazed, resulting in a network of hairline cracks. A contractor told me that the building must be given a waterproof coating to keep out water. Is this procedure really necessary?

No. The crackle of the glaze of architectural terra cotta is a result of the natural aging process and is relatively harmless. The amount of moisture absorbed through these fine cracks is negligible; the amount of evaporation through the cracks is probably as great as the amount of moisture absorbed. A waterproof or water-repellent coating would trap more moisture inside the terra cotta than it would keep out. Such coatings also have a relatively short life expectancy (three to five years) and can discolor a building. It would be better to spend this money on inspecting the building (especially the cornice, drains and so forth) and re-pointing the mortar joints where necessary.

Our church was constructed at the turn of the century of blocks made to look like cobblestone. We have been unable to find any information on this material. Can you tell us anything about it?

Concrete block, introduced in North America in the late 1860s, quickly became an inexpensive and popular building material. It frequently was designed to look like expensive stone, although rarely was it as durable. Blocks could be made to imitate many types of rough-cut or dressed stone, with or without tooling. Concrete block in a cobblestone pattern was often the choice for "country gothic" churches. Typically, the hollow units were made of concrete poured into a rigid mold; as soon as the mold had been filled, the block could be released and another begun. Although dimensions often varied, most blocks were 16 by 8 by 10 inches. A 1908 Sears, Roebuck catalog advertised a concrete building block machine, called "the Wizard," that promised a "perfect block in one minute's time." By the 1920s, as architectural styles changed, concrete block designed to look like stone ceased to be a popular building material.

I want to paint the gray stucco walls of my house an off-white. How should I prepare the surface?

Scrub the walls with water and a natural-bristle brush to remove any loose particles. After the walls dry, a paint recommended for stucco or cement can be applied. However, there is a disadvantage in painting stucco. If you want to restucco later, the new stucco will not properly adhere to the painted surface, and you will be forced to remove the old paint.

I have been told that stucco is a very durable exterior wall surface. Should I be concerned about the small cracks that have appeared in the stucco walls of my house?

Not necessarily. Hairline cracks on a stucco surface probably do not indicate a serious problem, but any larger cracks should be examined closely. If water can penetrate the wall, the crack must be repaired. One way to test for penetration is to tap lightly around the crack and listen for a hollow sound, which indicates that the bond of the stucco layer has broken. To patch the bond, follow a procedure recommended by a professional stucco contractor or supplier. This procedure will include removing loose material to a firm base—to the inner wall surface, if necessary—and patching with new material. You will generally find that only the outermost layer of the stucco is colored, and a careful match is necessary to blend the new work with the surrounding area. Because wet stucco is considerably darker, match colors when the materials are dry.

If a substantial amount of moisture has entered the wall for any length of time, some internal deterioration has probably occurred. In this case, the stucco should not be patched until the damage is corrected.

The wooden front of my shop dates from the turn of the century and is a distinctive feature of the building. I want to save it but do not know how to proceed. What do you suggest?

The key to preserving wooden storefronts is careful evaluation of existing physical conditions. Moisture, vandalism, insect attack and lack of maintenance can all contribute to the deterioration of wooden storefronts. Paint failure should not be interpreted as a sign that the wood is in poor condition and therefore unrepairable; wood beneath unsightly paint is frequently in sound condition. Using an ice pick or awl, test the wood for soundness by jabbing it—decayed wood will lift up in short, irregular pieces; sound wood will separate in long, fibrous splinters.

Storefronts showing signs of physical deterioration can often be repaired by simple methods. Partially decayed wood can be waterproofed, patched, built up or consolidated and then painted to achieve a sound condition, good appearance and greatly extended life.

To repair wood that is beginning to rot, it is advisable first to dry the wood and then treat decayed areas with a fungicide (a highly toxic substance). Waterproof with two or three applications of boiled linseed oil, allowing 24 hours' drying time between applications. Then fill cracks and holes with putty, caulk the joints between the various wooden members and, finally, prime and paint the surface.

Partially decayed wood can also be strengthened and stabilized by consolidation, using semirigid epoxies that saturate porous decayed wood and then harden. The consolidated wood can then be filled with a semirigid epoxy patching compound, sanded and painted.

When components of wooden storefronts are so badly deteriorated that they cannot be stabilized, it may be possible to replace the deteriorated parts by patching in new pieces or by splicing new wood into existing members. These techniques all require skill and some expense but are recommended when decorative elements are involved. In some cases, missing edges can be filled and rebuilt with wood putty or epoxy compounds. When the epoxy cures, it can be sanded smooth and painted to achieve a durable and waterproof surface.

We are rehabilitating a two-and-a-half-story frame house that dates from 1900. The contractor has advised us to remodel the structure so that it will be less costly to maintain—for example, the wood porch has required repairs on several occasions, and the clapboard and porch always seem to be in need of paint. Plans so far include removing the porch and installing 4-inch aluminum siding over the clapboards. Is this an appropriate approach?

Your contractor's proposal is not an acceptable way to rehabilitate your house. Your house's architectural character is most likely based on the use of wood for both structural and decorative purposes. Elimination of the porch, narrow novelty siding and decorative bargeboards would irreversibly alter the house. It is strongly recommended that you retain these features through continued maintenance and repair.

If wood surfaces are properly prepared for painting and then painted with a high-quality exterior paint, you should be able to relax for five to eight years. If the porch flashing, gutters, roofing, and joint and seam caulking are kept in a proper state of repair, deterioration should be minimal. In the future, should any part of the porch require replacement, wood rather than substitute materials is recommended. As for placing aluminum or vinyl siding on top of your present clapboard, incorrect installation could lead to moisture problems, which are in the long run far more costly than planned maintenance.

ALUMINUM SIDING   ORIGINAL CLAPBOARD

We need to repaint the exterior of our clapboard house, which already has several coats of paint. A local contractor has recommended sandblasting to remove all the paint, leaving only the bare wood. What are the pros and cons of this procedure?

There are no pros. Sandblasting erodes the soft, porous fibers (spring wood) faster than the hard, dense fibers (summer wood), leaving a pitted surface with ridges and valleys. It also erodes projecting areas of carvings and moldings before it removes paint from concave areas, so that paint residue often has to be removed by hand.

Besides its obvious detrimental effect on any architectural detailing, sandblasting causes the wood to become so porous—much like bare, naturally weathered wood—that considerably more paint is required to cover the surface, thus creating an economic problem as well. In short, you would be much better off exploring other methods of paint removal, particularly use of an electric heat plate. If parts of the painted surface of your house have not cracked or peeled to the bare wood, they probably can be scraped and sanded down to the next sound paint layer and then repainted.

A contractor has assured me that water-blasting can get rid of layers of old, cracked paint on my exterior wood siding. Do you recommend this procedure, and, if not, what other method can I consider?

Waterblasting is not recommended because it can force water into the wood rather than—or in addition to—removing paint. In high-pressure waterblasting the pressure can sometimes reach as high as 2,000 pounds per square inch and can cause the water to penetrate exterior sheathing and damage interior finishes. For the gentlest abrasive method using water, use a detergent solution, scrub with a medium-soft bristle brush and use a garden hose for rinsing. This method is recommended when cleaning intact exterior surfaces before repainting, for removing chalking paint or just as an annual preservation practice to remove dirt and organic debris.

In the case of your old, cracked paint, you may be successful in removing damaged paint layers down to a sound layer with a putty knife or paint scraper. This process should be followed by sanding (either by hand or with an orbital sander) to feather or smooth the remaining paint so that all layers are uniformly attached before repainting. Because your house most likely has oil paint on it now, you should use a high-quality exterior oil paint again.

If, on the other hand, the paint on your siding has cracked down to bare wood and failure is extensive, you will probably need to use an electric heat plate and wide-bladed scraper for total paint removal. After scraping, sand lightly, coat the bare wood with an oil primer within 48 hours and then repaint with a compatible oil or latex finish paint.

Is there a safe substitute for water-repellent preservatives that contain pentachlorophenol? I want to apply a coat to a new wooden window sash for my 1910 house before painting it.

If you do not mind mixing your own formula from scratch, you can prepare a safe substance for above-ground wood products. The U.S. Department of Agriculture's Forest Products Laboratory comparatively tested wooden window units dipped for three minutes in a solution of water-repellent preservative containing pentachlorophenol and window units dipped in a simple water-repellent mixture without the chemical preservative. The units were then exposed to the weather for 20 years. The results showed that the condition of the window units that had been dipped in the plain water-repellent mixture was as good as those dipped in the chemical preservative. (Window units that received no treatment at all literally fell apart after six years' exposure.)

The Forest Products Laboratory maintains that a water-repellent treatment without the addition of a preservative can provide excellent decay resistance to outdoor woodwork. This kind of treatment can save money and resources and is a preservative-free method of maintaining birdhouses, sheds, porch and fence rails and other above-ground wood structures.

The Forest Products Laboratory's recommended formula is as follows: Mix 3 cups exterior varnish and 1 ounce paraffin wax; add mineral spirits, paint thinner or turpentine to make I gallon. This treatment can be applied before or after construction and before painting. The wood should be dipped in the solution for one to three minutes. If dipping is not convenient, apply liberally with a brush, paying particular attention to heavy treatment of all board ends and joints. The treated surface can then be painted after two or three days of warm weather. Paint should last longer on a treated surface than on an untreated surface.

LOG HOUSE WITH CLAPBOARD SIDING

LOG HOUSE WITH EXPOSED LOGS

We would like to expose the logs on the historic log house we have purchased, but we have heard that removing the clapboard siding and the interior plaster is not a good idea. Why not?

Many log houses have survived, some for more than 200 years, because most were protected on the outside with siding or shingles. Although custom varied from region to region, log houses usually were considered less prestigious than frame or brick houses and were often covered with clapboard siding soon after they were built.

Siding was used for practical reasons. It made the house less drafty and protected the logs. The irregular spaces between the logs were filled with chinking (wood chips, stones, moss or whatever was available) and daubing (mud mortar that consisted of dirt and perhaps some lime, if available). Often the daubing crumbled when it dried or was washed away by driving rain. The daubing had to be patched annually because most log houses did not have sufficient eave overhang to protect the logs. Plaster on the inside made the house easier to keep clean, allowed such amenities as painted or wallpapered walls and made the house less drafty, in addition to providing some additional insulation value.

In the 20th century, some log houses were built with portland cement mortar, which is harder and more durable than mud mortar. In general, these houses have deteriorated much faster than earlier log houses because the logs have been exposed to the elements and because portland cement mortar shrinks when it cures, leaving hairline cracks between the mortar and the logs. Once moisture enters these cracks, the logs begin to rot.

Removal of the siding and plaster, in addition to being historically incorrect, may also be physically detrimental to the structure. Even if you accept the maintenance problem of patching the mud mortar, the logs are still exposed to the weather. Modern waterproof coatings have generally proved to be ineffective, lasting only two to three years, often trapping moisture and darkening the logs or giving them a glossy, unnatural appearance.

I own an old adobe house in New Mexico that dates from the 1890s. The exterior portion of several of the vigas is beginning to rot. Is there a way to repair these logs, or must I replace them with new logs?

Exterior projecting vigas are structural and design elements intrinsic to the character of historic adobe buildings; thus, every effort should be made to preserve them as original features. If the deterioration process is not arrested quickly, the decay may spread through the logs, and the structurally unsound vigas may cause partial or total collapse of the roof.

It may be possible to stabilize the vigas (if they have not deteriorated too much), using a wood epoxy compound. Epoxy can be applied to the vigas to fill in any cracks and voids in the wood. The hardened epoxy can be sanded or planed down in the shape of the viga and can then be painted. You will probably want to hire an expert to carry out the work.

Of course, if some of the vigas have deteriorated too much, they may have to be partially or totally replaced with new wood. Do not replace the vigas with false projections. It is almost impossible to attach false vigas securely; hence, the solution they provide is not only a temporary one but also a potentially dangerous one, because vigas are often used as support in gaining access to the roof.

The carpenter repairing the porch on our Queen Anne house told us that the floor boards are suffering from "dry rot." I have always been confused about what this term means. Please explain.

The term "dry rot" is a misnomer because the fungi that cause decay must have access to water in order to grow. Even though the wood may be dry when the "rot" is detected, it must first have been wet in order to decay. Most rot occurs in wood when its moisture content is above the fiber saturation point, or 30 percent moisture content.

The sawn-wood ornamentation on the porch and along the cornice of our small Victorian cottage has missing pieces and is broken in places. What is the best approach to restoring this important feature of the house?

Each section and piece of the sawn-wood ornamentation should be examined to determine what can be repaired and what must be replaced. In many cases, only the small or more delicate edge portions of the ornamentation may be broken, and they can be reconstructed by gluing into place new wood and repairing with epoxy resin and fillers, as needed. If a section is completely beyond repair, it can be "cannibalized"—that is, used to piece another section. When entire pieces or sections are missing, it is usually a relatively simple process to shape new ones with a saber or jigsaw and a portable drill with a hole-cutter attachment. You may need to have the wood milled to match exactly the width and thickness of the original wood, or perhaps the local mill could make all the sawn-wood ornamentation for you. Another alternative would be to check with various national suppliers of new wood ornamentation for old houses to see if your missing pieces are carried in stock.

Is wisteria likely to harm the wooden shingle siding of my Cape May, N.J., cottage? If so, what is the best way to remove it?

Although walls covered by wisteria are aesthetically pleasing, the vines should be removed because they can force shingles apart or cause them to crack and pop off. The wood also absorbs water retained in the plants, and the excessive moisture could cause rot fungi.

The best way to remove wisteria is to cut the plant at its base and paint the stumps with a commercially available tree-root killer. After the plants dry and shrink, remove the vegetation by hand.

Herbicides should not be sprayed directly on buildings, except in cases where the plants cannot be removed by hand (for example, poison ivy). Steam and hot-water spray introduce too much moisture into the wood.

Because weather conditions in Cape May cause wood to deteriorate, you should remove the vines as soon as possible. Replace any damaged shingles and apply a wood preservative-fungicide to protect them from further deterioration.

I have been told that the window hoods and cornice of the late 19th-century brick row house I am planning to purchase may be metal, although I had assumed they were stone. How can I find out whether they are stone or metal?

Many decorative architectural features on mid-19th-century to early 20th-century buildings, such as window and door moldings, appear from a distance to be masonry or wood but are actually pressed sheet metal, often coated with zinc. Sheet metal was, of course, much lighter, less expensive and easier to install than stone. If well maintained and painted, these metal elements successfully imitate stone or wood. However, when the paint begins to peel, the silvery gray color of the metal reveals its true identity.

Paint does not adhere well to pure zinc or to galvanized iron or steel. When paint peels, usually all of it comes off, including the primer, to reveal a clean metal surface. If the metal is galvanized, it will have a spangled appearance and may show some rust from the iron base metal. If the metal is cast or pressed zinc, it will have a grayish white appearance.

With the help of a ladder and a magnet, you can identify painted metal architectural elements; the magnet will adhere to galvanized iron or steel but not to pure zinc, which is non-magnetic. If the building has not been properly maintained and the paint has worn off, the zinc coating on iron may have oxidized, leaving whitish corrosion stains.

To prepare for repainting, scrape all surfaces to remove loose zinc carbonate and re-caulk or resolder joints. Finally, repaint the metal using a zinc chromate primer and a high-quality exterior oil paint.

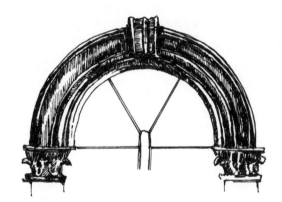

The decorative metal storefront on my building has been covered with many coats of paint. I want to restore it to its original appearance but do not know how to proceed. Can you help me?

Storefronts were fabricated from a variety of metals, including cast iron, bronze, copper, stainless steel, tin, galvanized sheet iron and cast zinc. Before steps can be taken to analyze or treat deteriorated storefronts, it is necessary to know which metals are involved, for each has unique properties and distinct preservation treatments. Determining metal composition can be a difficult process, and an architectural consultant should be retained to help with this type of work. Cast iron and iron alloys are perhaps the easiest to detect—simply use a magnet.

When paint buildup and rust are not severe problems, hand scraping and wirebrushing are suitable cleaning methods. Although it is necessary to remove all rust before repainting, it is not necessary to remove all paint. In cases of extensive paint buildup and corrosion, gentle mechanical methods such as low-pressure, dry-grit blasting (80–100 pounds per square inch) can be an effective and economical cleaning method and provide a good surface for paint. Masonry and wood surfaces adjacent to the cleaning area, however, should be protected to avoid inadvertent damage from the blasting. It will be necessary to recaulk and putty heads of screws and bolts after grit blasting to prevent moisture from entering the joints. Immediately after cleaning, paint the cleaned areas with a rust-inhibiting primer to prevent new corrosion.

Storefronts made of softer metals (lead and tin), sheet metals (sheet copper) and plated metals (tin and terneplate) should not be cleaned mechanically because their finish can be easily abraded and damaged. These softer metals preferably should be cleaned with a chemical method (acid pickling or phosphate dipping) or a thermal method. Again, after cleaning the surface of the metal of all corrosion, grease and dirt, apply a rust-inhibiting primer coat. Finish coats especially formulated for metals, consisting of lacquers, varnishes, enamels or special coatings, can be applied once the primer has dried.

The proper restoration of metal storefronts should not be considered a do-it-yourself project. The nature and condition of the material should be assessed by a competent professional and the work conducted by a specialized company.

My partner and I are rehabilitating a four-story commercial building with a cast-iron facade. Many of its decorative features, such as acanthus leaves and rosettes on the cornice modillions, are missing. Our contractor suggested that these missing parts be reproduced in fiber glass or aluminum. Is this substitution an acceptable practice?

Both aluminum and fiber glass can be successfully used as substitute materials for replacing missing cast-iron decorative elements. Aluminum shrinks in the curing process at a rate of about ⅜ inch per foot; therefore, this shrinkage must be taken into account, and all patterns must be larger than the original. Aluminum, when used, must be isolated from the cast-iron components by nonporous, neoprene gaskets or butyl rubber caulking (or both) to avoid galvanic corrosion. Fiber-glass elements can be made from a latex mold of the existing cast-iron pieces because fiber glass shrinks in the curing process only at a rate of ¹⁄₁₆ inch per foot; therefore, this shrinking should have no effect on small replacement parts such as rosettes and acanthus leaves. Fiber glass deteriorates, however, if exposed to the ultraviolet rays of the sun and consequently must be kept painted.

We are renovating our Victorian property and need advice on cleaning the cast-iron fence and foliated porch railing. The fence has quite a bit of rust, but the porch railing has only a little rust. We also have to replace a few pieces of ornamentation missing from the porch railing. Do you have any suggestions?

You might want to consider two types of cleaning—one for the fence and another for the porch railing. Dry sandblasting, if your city permits it, may be an economical way to clean your fence because it requires only a minimum amount of preparation. Any shrubbery should be covered for protection during sandblasting, and gauge pressure, to avoid pitting the cast iron, should not exceed 80–100 pounds per square inch. The operator also should be fully protected with safety equipment. To reduce the dust often created by sandblasting, city codes may allow only waterblasting. However, water will compound the rusting problem of the fence; moreover, the fence is made up of many parts, and it is too difficult to ensure that the iron is completely dry before the fence is primed. For these two reasons, you should consider mechanical cleaning.

Mechanical scraping would be most appropriate for your porch railing because there is not much rusting and the use of sandblasting equipment would require masking all the adjacent masonry and wooden material. Electric drills have special wire-brush and rotary-whip attachments that remove rust and flaking paint from cast iron. The operator should wear protective goggles and safety equipment to avoid the small fragments that will fly off the metal. Some sanding by hand in the corners where the rotary equipment cannot reach may be necessary.

It will not be necessary to remove all the paint if it is well bonded. However, all the rusted and flaking areas should be cleaned down to the bare metal to ensure that corrosion will not continue. The bare metal should be primed within four hours with a rust-inhibiting oil primer followed by a second coat of primer and two top coats of high-quality exterior oil paint. The primer and finish paint should be manufactured by the same company to ensure compatibility.

To find a source for replacing the missing cast-iron pieces, check with your local ironworks or foundry or a restoration products catalog (see Reading About Rehabilitation).

Is sandblasting a cost-effective way to clean the industrial rolled steel windows in my brick warehouse building? The windows have quite a bit of rust but no major structural damage, although all the glass has been broken by vandals.

Because you are undertaking a major renovation of the windows and because there is no glass to be saved, sandblasting your metal windows will be cost effective. However, you must provide proper protective shields for the masonry surrounds of the windows to ensure that the brick is not abraded by the sandblasting. Gauge pressure should not exceed 80–100 pounds per square inch. You may find the small, nozzled "pencil" blasters effective in cleaning all the dried putty from around the glazing channels. The pressure from the sandblasting also will remove any caulking or putty covering recessed screws or bolts, so caulking will have to be replaced as part of the window repair.

If waterblasting is used, the window sections should be blown dry immediately and primed within four hours or the metal will begin to rust. An oil primer with an anticorrosive agent should be used, and the finish coats should be a high-quality exterior oil paint manufactured by the same company to ensure compatibility. All local environmental and safety codes should be followed carefully.

How do I prepare steel casement windows for repainting, and what kind of paint should I use? A small amount of rusting is visible under the flaking paint on the bottom section of the windows.

You will probably need to brush the flaking paint with a stiff brush and then use a phosphoric acid gel formulated to remove rust. Follow the manufacturer's instructions for using the chemical rust remover, and remember to avoid letting water mixed with chemicals come in contact with the glass or the masonry sills and surrounds of the window. It is better to rinse off the chemical with clean, damp cloths than with running water. Once the rust and flaking paint are removed, the windows should be primed with an appropriate primer and finish coats of paint. Red-lead primers are not available for residential use because of their toxicity; zinc-rich primers are an effective alternative, although they should be used carefully because they are toxic substances. The finish coats should be a high-quality exterior oil paint that is compatible with the rust-inhibiting primer.

I own a townhouse that dates from the 1870s and am trying to replace missing hardware with appropriate period hardware. I have found a beautiful solid brass door knob for a mortise lock. Now I need to know what door knockers were customarily made of at the end of the 19th century. The "ghost mark" on the door indicates that the original door knocker was a simple, rectangular shape.

You should try to duplicate as closely as possible the size and shape of the original door knocker. A well-known hardware catalog of 1865 produced by the Russell and Erwin Manufacturing Company (now available in reprint) lists several choices of materials and finishes that would be suitable for your front door. Depending on the amount of money you want to spend, you could choose from among these historic materials and finishes: solid brass, brass plate, or "French bronzed" or Japanned brass plate. You can look for reproductions of these in restoration products catalogs, find a craftsman to fashion a special reproduction or attempt to locate a similar original in an architectural salvage shop.

The bronze grille at the entrance to our neoclassical bank has acquired a greenish patina. What causes patina? Does it provide protection against corrosion?

Patina is the natural corrosion that occurs on the surface of outdoor bronzes. It varies in color from green to black. For many years patina was thought to provide protection against further corrosion, but whether it does so depends on how the patina is formed and whether it is soluble in its environment. If the patina is formed uniformly and adheres tightly to the surface of the bronze to form an impervious coating, it will usually protect the metal from further corrosion. On the other hand, some corrosive products are porous and permit corrosion to continue deeper and deeper. Factors that probably influence how the patina is formed are wind patterns, rain, surface dirt and soot, industrial pollution and bird droppings. In addition, if the patina is soluble in rain and the rain is contaminated with dissolved chemicals, the patina will offer little protection. When the patina washes away, fresh metal is exposed; it corrodes, is dissolved and washes away again. If this cycle is repeated many times, a significant loss of material can result. To complicate matters, the porosity and solubility of the patina may vary from spot to spot on one piece of bronze.

Severe pitting and obvious loss of material from corrosion are good indications that the patina is not protective. There are no simple tests to confirm this condition. A bronze conservator should be retained to diagnose the situation and prescribe a conservation treatment.

ROOFS AND ROOFING

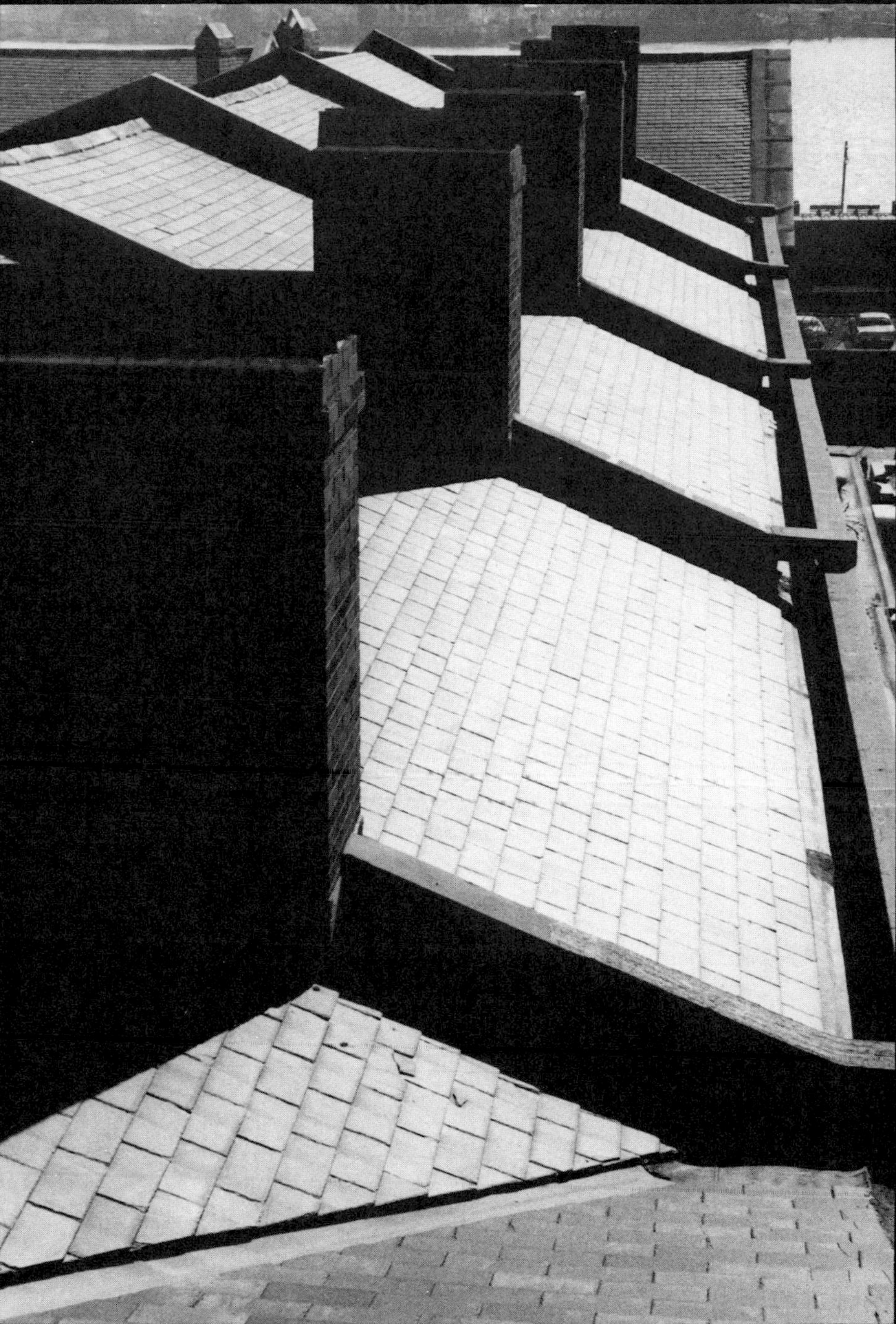

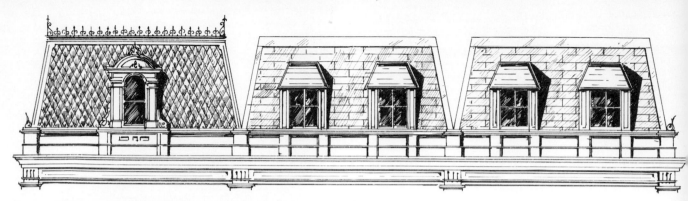

I own three adjacent Victorian row houses that I intend to rehabilitate for office use. Although the mansard roofs were once identical, some features have been changed over the years so that only one of the houses retains its original patterned slate roof and segmental arched dormer. The roofs of the other two houses were covered about 40 years ago with asphalt shingles, and the single dormers were replaced with double hipped-roof dormers. The slate and the original dormer need repair. What approach should I take to make the roofs of the three buildings harmonious?

Because the buildings have not been identical for many years, you should not feel obligated to reconstruct an appearance that does not exist. But you should always save original or significant historic fabric. One approach would be to retain and restore the roofing and dormers on the other two houses to match. However, if this option is too expensive, you should simply repair the newer dormers and asphalt shingles, because rehabilitation does not require reconstruction of lost features.

I am the building manager of an 1895 courthouse. I am considering having an asphalt roofing compound applied to the copper roof to keep it watertight. The courthouse is in a historic district, and I want to be sure that what I am doing will be appropriate.

This method is unnecessary for a copper roof because copper is fairly resistant to corrosion caused by moisture. It is more prone to damage from erosion, thermal expansion and contraction, improper fastenings and an insufficient substructure. The asphalt roofing compound may, in fact, corrode the copper, because some bituminous compounds (asphalt is one kind) have been known to attack copper. Many of these compounds will melt slightly when exposed to the sun and, if applied to a pitched roof, may run off the roof and down the sides of the building. These compounds are better suited to fairly low-pitched, asphalt felt-rolled roofs.

Also, any change in the roof color (which would occur if you applied the asphalt coating to your roof, painted or not), would produce a radical change in the courthouse's appearance. Such changes should, thus, be carefully weighed against the long-term maintenance considerations.

In the last several years sections of the copper roof of our church have had to be replaced. The old copper roof is green, but the new copper is almost as bright as a new penny. As a result, the roof looks blotchy and unattractive. Should we paint the new copper green to match the old?

It takes 8 to 10 years for copper to weather from bright copper to brown to black and, finally, to green. If you paint the new copper, it will never weather to form a natural patina under the paint, and it will have to be repainted about every five years. Repainting the roof is a needless, expensive maintenance cost.

Of course, the least expensive solution would be to allow the new copper to acquire its patina naturally. A green patina can be obtained through chemical application, although this color may not perfectly match the old copper because natural patina has a streaked look. If more than half of the roof was replaced, it may be less expensive to clean the old copper to a bright appearance and let both the old and new copper develop a natural patina at the same time. For further information on copper patina, as well as brass and bronze patina, contact the Copper Development Association, 405 Lexington Avenue, New York, N.Y. 10017.

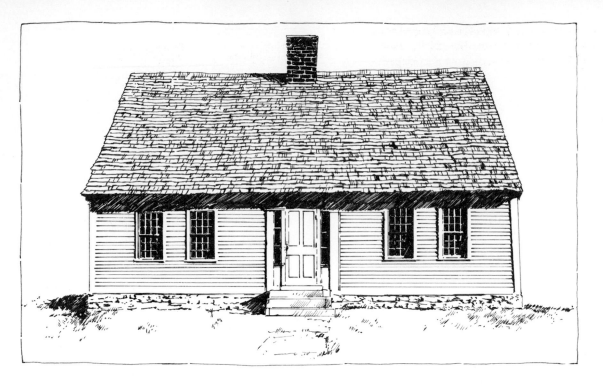

We have recently repaired our brick fireplace and now use it regularly. Our roof is made of wooden shingles, and we are concerned about the risk of fire. Can the shingles be coated to make them fire retardant?

To protect your wood-shingle roof, you should first install a screen above the flue to catch sparks. Also, you can protect the shingles themselves—for example, by painting them with a fire-retardant paint. If the roof needs to be replaced, you may wish to install new fire-retardant (pressure-impregnated) wooden shingles, which are often guaranteed for 20 years.

If you decide to treat the existing shingles, two types of coatings are suitable—penetrating clear liquids and epoxy paints. In a fire, the epoxy paints intumesce—that is, expand or foam — thus providing a thermal barrier to the fire and protecting the wood from combustion.

Both types of coating have serious limitations. The fire retardant should be viewed as a paint layer just like that on siding or other exterior wooden elements. It is affected by sun, rain and wind and must be renewed (repainted) about every three years. Also, either type of coating might change the appearance of the roof.

On the positive side, the coatings tend to lengthen the life of the shingle roof because they include certain preservatives and reduce the potential for moisture deterioration of the wood.

When choosing a coating, ask for exterior fire-retardant paints; there are several brands. Contact a number of local paint dealers and compare the cost and durability of the coatings and the consumer report ratings of the products. Painting a roof can be dangerous, so you will probably want to contract the work rather than do it yourself. Always get at least three estimates and inquire about the reputation of the contractor.

Our old house has roof moisture problems. We would like to install new flashing, but we have heard that aluminum is susceptible to corrosion. Is this true? If so, what are the best materials to use for flashing, and where should it be placed to ensure maximum protection?

Although aluminum is thought of as a metal that is resistant to most types of corrosion, it is susceptible to some corrosive agents, such as lead paints, hydrochloric acid, alkalis, chlorides and certain wood preservatives. Moisture accumulation and high humidity levels cause aluminum to deteriorate quickly; it corrodes when it comes in contact with damp brick, stonework and unseasoned damp wood shingles. Aluminum flashing can be used successfully if it is protected by insulative coatings such as paint, mastics or plastic. When attaching the flashing, fasten it only with aluminum nails; in this way, contact with corrosive agents is prevented.

Flashing and counterflashing should be placed on anything that protrudes through or abuts the roof, including chimneys, valleys, dormers, eaves, window heads and cornices. Flashing installed in these areas should extend 7 to 10 inches up both sides of the valley, protrusion, roofline or whatever area is being protected.

In America in the 18th century lead was often used as a flashing material. Copper also has been widely used, and many experts still believe that it is the best material for flashing. Plastic can be used as a flashing material in selected areas, such as under window sills and heads.

HANDSPLIT SHAKE   SAWN SHINGLE

My husband and I want to put back a wood-shingle roof on our 18th-century house, but we disagree about the appropriate style of shingle to use. My husband wants to use a modern handsplit shake, but I prefer the more regular appearance of sawn shingles. Please advise.

Most shingle, or "shake," roofs on modest and substantial dwellings during the 18th century were made of handsplit shingles. The faces of shingles were then dressed—that is, smoothed—to reduce the unevenness caused by the splitting of the wood, to improve the general visual qualities and, in particular, to make the roof more weathertight. The modern handsplit shake, which is not dressed, is much too rough in appearance when compared with the shingles of most 18th-century roofs that have survived. The cheapest and most practical way to approximate the historic appearance is to use a premium-grade sawn shingle.

My late 19th-century house needs a new roof. My contractor advised me that when the roof is replaced, the old wooden built-in gutter should be covered over and an aluminum gutter attached to the face of the cornice. Is it really impractical to make old gutters functional again? I want to save the appearance of my cornice.

Hanging gutters can have a negative visual effect on the cornices of old houses. Built-in gutters are often referred to as "concealed" gutters, and, as their name suggests, one of their advantages is that they are not easily visible. In many cases such gutters help form the historic cornice and were located sufficiently far from the outer wall that any eventual water leakage would not penetrate and damage interior walls.

As with gutter systems in general, a built-in gutter must be maintained and routinely checked for debris. The basic design of built-in gutters is usually sound; in fact, they are still used today in new construction and are especially common in the Northeast. You may find it necessary to repair or replace portions of the wooden gutter; in most cases the wooden gutter's metal lining fails first. If the old liner needs to be completely replaced, most roofers would recommend using lead-coated copper. Perhaps your contractor does not want to be bothered with repairing the old gutters; if so, you might want to get several other opinions from experienced roofers.

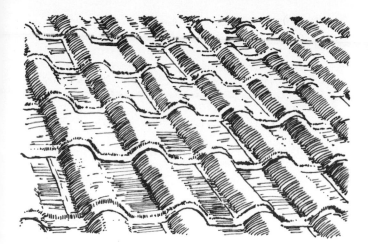

The roof on a building I own is covered with Spanish clay tiles that are deteriorated; many have fallen off, and others are severely cracked. Estimates from roofing contractors for replacing the clay tiles are very high, although I realize that such a roof lasts a long time and may be cost effective in the long run. Because few of the tiles can be salvaged, I want to find a substitute roofing material that is less expensive and also looks like the original S-shaped tiles. What do you suggest?

Perhaps you should consider replacing the clay tiles (called pantiles) with galvanized metal shingles. These shingles, which imitate the appearance of pantiles, were traditionally used in the 19th and early 20th centuries as a substitute for clay tiles. They were produced in a variety of styles and included special ridge, valley and hip pieces. After the galvanized metal shingles have been installed, they can be painted with a color approximating that of the original clay tiles. To our knowledge, only one company in the country still manufactures galvanized metal shingles that look like Spanish clay tiles, using original dies in the stamping (W.F. Norman Corporation, Box 323, 214 North Cedar Street, Nevada, Mo. 64772).

Last year we converted a 50-year-old passenger station into a library. The project turned out beautifully, except for one problem — the Spanish tile roof continues to leak even though it has been repaired repeatedly. Is there a product we can spray on the tiles that would hold them in place and seal them together?

Unfortunately, there is no miracle product that can be sprayed on the tiles to seal them and prevent leaks. Moreover, although clay tiles can last a long time, they are an inherently fragile roofing material. They cannot support much weight and, if stepped on carelessly, may crack or break. Also, incorrect anchoring or attachment methods may cause tiles to break and may destroy the integrity of the roofing system as a waterproof membrane protecting the interior of the building.

You could ask a roofing contractor who has not been previously involved in your project to carry out an impartial investigation of the leaking roof and make recommendations for its repair.

The contractor who is restoring our colonial farmhouse claims that the windows are not repairable, but much of the wood looks fine. How can we determine whether the windows can be repaired?

A basic rule of preservation is to retain as much original building fabric as possible—including windows. Original windows are an integral part of the house and help shape its style and appearance. Moreover, the quality of the wood in older windows is often better than that of new windows. And, finally, retaining old windows can sometimes be less expensive than purchasing and installing new ones.

For the contractor, replacing the windows is usually easier and, therefore, more profitable than repairing them, but every effort should be made to retain windows that are in good condition or that can be repaired. Peeling paint, loose putty and broken sash cords are not indications that windows have been damaged irreparably. All too often, historic window sash are removed when, in fact, little more work than scraping, painting and weatherstripping is needed. A quick method of determining whether the fabric is salvageable is the ice-pick test. If the pick penetrates the wood less than one-eighth of an inch, the wood is solid. If the pick penetrates the wood a half inch or more, the wood possibly has dry rot. Deterioration is more common on the bottom rail of the sash and at corner joints or intersections of muntins, where rain or condensation may collect, so check these areas first. If you find some rot, all is not lost. New pieces can be made. And replacing a few bottom rails will be less expensive than replacing all the windows.

I have insulated the attic and crawl space of my house, and now I am trying to decide how to reduce energy lost through my windows. Should I use storm windows or buy new, double-glazed replacement windows?

Installing storm windows is preferable to installing new windows for several reasons in addition to the principle that original windows should be retained whenever possible. First, windows in historic houses often contribute to the architectural character and probably fit the wall openings better than new units, especially if the building has undergone uneven settlement. Second, the wood in the frame and sash is a far better insulator than metal, which is frequently used in replacement windows.

Storm windows are an economical way to achieve double-glazing and thereby improve the thermal performance of windows. For the owner of a historic house, storm windows can be installed with minimal damage to the window and can be easily removed. Storm windows are made for either interior or exterior application and are available in a variety of frame materials. From the standpoint of energy efficiency, exterior storm windows are preferred, although they may have greater visual impact. Interior storm windows can be hidden by curtains or draperies, but greater care must be taken with them to prevent moisture buildup in the air space. Such moisture can condense on the outer prime windows and could lead to the deterioration of paint or wood. Interior storm windows should be thoroughly sealed to prevent room air from leaking into the air space, and the outer window should be loose enough to allow moisture to bleed off into the outside air.

We are renovating our Victorian house, which has large, one-over-one, double-hung wooden windows. During the renovation, while the windows are out of their frames, we want to replace the dried and cracked putty. Should we use putty or glazing compound in reglazing?

Both will work, but putty is recommended for wooden windows. Glazing compound, generally an acrylic latex product, was primarily developed for glazing metal windows. It has a soft, workable consistency, sets up within 24 hours and remains flexible; however, it will not form the tight seal necessary to prevent water penetration and subsequent wood deterioration.

Putty, which has a boiled linseed oil base, was developed especially for glazing wooden windows. The advantage of putty is that it forms a tight seal with the wood; a disadvantage is that it tends to creep if large windows are reglazed in place. However, since you plan to remove the sash during renovation, creeping putty should not be a problem. Lay the windows flat while applying the putty, and let them dry flat for a week. Incidentally, when removing the old putty, clean the rabbet and lubricate the raw wood channel with boiled linseed oil before reglazing to further ensure a good seal.

Last autumn we put weatherstripping on our double-hung windows, but this spring we could not get the windows open without removing or damaging the weatherstripping. How can weatherstripping be installed so that it will last several years and still allow the windows to be operable?

Most double-hung windows are designed for both the upper and lower sash to move; therefore, weatherstripping must not hinder this movement. Weatherstripping can be composed of a variety of materials and installed at several points along the window frame: (1) Wood weatherstripping with a felt edge can be nailed on the lower half of the inside of the window frame along the interior stops and the sill, not attached to the sash; (2) metal weatherstripping with a rubber bead edge can be installed on the upper half of the window frame along the exterior stops and the head, not attached to the sash; (3) a felt strip can be stapled to the top edge of the upper sash or (4) a felt strip can be stapled to the inside edge of the meeting rail of the upper sash.

When the window is locked, the felt on the meeting rail is compressed and seals off the crack between the meeting rails of the upper and lower sash. The felt, in turn, pushes the two sash against the stops and the weatherstripping, thus sealing the cracks on all sides. When the window is unlocked, the meeting rails do not touch and the sash are free to move easily. The felt strip on the top of the upper sash seals the crack at the top of the window, creating a snug fit. A felt strip in the bottom of the lower sash is not advisable because it tends to "wick up" water and keeps it in contact with the sill and sash, providing ideal conditions for rot. Properly installed, weatherstripping should last at least 10 years.

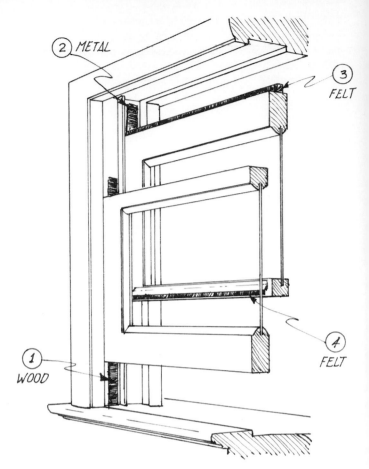

Our house, built about 1929 of English Tudor design, has steel casement windows that are no longer tight and leak air at the point where the movable window meets the frame. We have tried using the tacky-backed weatherstripping sold at hardware stores, but it does not adhere well to the steel. We would prefer not to install interior or exterior storm windows because of the aesthetic value of the casement windows. Can you suggest a way of sealing the windows against the casement that would eliminate drafts of air coming through the cracks but still permit the window to be opened in the spring and fall?

Thin spring-bronze weatherstripping for your steel casement windows would be preferable to the thick foam type you are using. Thick weatherstripping tends to spring the hinges, further warping the casement sash.

Spring-bronze weatherstripping can be purchased with an integral U-shaped flange that fits over the fixed metal frame and is held in place by a friction fit. First, weatherstrip three sides of the frame, leaving the hinge side alone. Sometimes the thickness of the weatherstripping will have a wedging effect on the hinge side, providing a tight seal. To test the effectiveness of the weatherstripping, on a windy day pass a lighted candle or "smoke pencil" around the perimeter of the closed window. If the hinge side is not properly closed, the flame will flicker and the smoke will drift away, indicating air penetration. In this case, weatherstripping should be added to the hinge side as well.

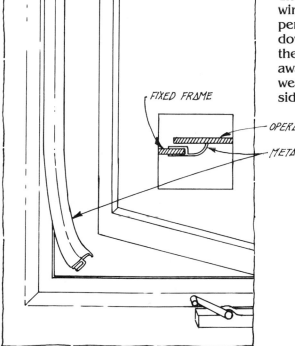

FIXED FRAME

OPERABLE WINDOW

METAL WEATHERSTRIPPING

How can rooms with bay windows be kept warm? Although I have installed storm windows and have caulked and weather-stripped the windows, these rooms are still colder than the rest of my house.

These rooms are so cold in the winter because of the large area of window and because glass is an excellent conductor. Consider installing thermal shutters and shades on the inside. Depending on the window's size, condition and orientation and on the type of shutters and shades chosen, heat loss can be reduced by 30 to 70 percent.

There are many types of thermal shutters and shades. Some can be easily constructed by the house owner with inexpensive but effective insulating materials, such as fiber glass, polyester quilting and Styrofoam. These materials are sometimes combined with mylar or aluminum foil to lessen heat loss through radiation. Shades are flexible so that they can be rolled up when not needed. Shutters are hinged at the side and folded back when not in use.

Many new shutters and shades are suitable for historic buildings, because they can be attached—or removed—with little or no damage to the building. Although many are custom-made and thus fit the shapes of older windows, they can be relatively inexpensive.

We have storm windows that clip into the inside frame of our 45-year-old wooden casement windows. The windows seem to constantly steam up in the winter. What can we do to prevent this?

This problem is a common one with many storm window-prime window combinations. Although it probably cannot be entirely eliminated, it can be considerably lessened. The steam is caused when the warm, moist interior air seeps into the space between the storm and the prime window and condenses on the cold, outermost window (the prime window). First, try reducing the amount of moisture in the air; this is a problem, especially if you have a humidifier. Second, reduce the condensation problem itself by ensuring the tightest possible seal between the storm window and the prime sash; usually, adding foam weatherstripping between the two will help. Always be sure to wipe up the excess moisture frequently, temporarily removing the storm sash. Finally, a sound coat of paint on the prime sash ensures minimal moisture damage to the wood.

The front window of my store is in pretty good shape, but the glass has cracked and the putty has dried out. How should I tackle the problem?

Glass windows are generally the most prominent features of historic storefronts, so they should be properly maintained. For wooden frames, remove deteriorated putty manually, taking care not to damage wood along the rabbet. To reglaze, lay a bead of putty around the perimeter of the rabbet, press the panel into place, insert glazing points to hold the pane, and bevel a final seal of putty around the edge of the glass. For metal-frame windows, use glazing compound and special glazing clips to secure the glass and then apply a final seal of glazing compound. If the glass needs replacing, the new glass should match the original in size, color and reflective qualities.

The front door of my 80-year-old house is made of a beautiful hardwood with raised paneling. The problem is that the porcelain door knobs are broken and the rimlock no longer functions properly. Because I am worried about vandalism, I have been thinking about replacing the entire door and hardware with a new steel security door. What is your advice?

The description of your front door and hardware indicates that they are important features of your house because of the prominence of the design and the authenticity of the materials. Replacement porcelain knobs are relatively easy to find; they can either be salvaged from old buildings or reproduced. The rimlock should be repaired, if possible, or similarly replaced with another old rimlock or a reproduction. The primary consideration in the security of your front door is not the material of the door itself, but the strength of the elements that keep it closed. For security, add a dead bolt lock.

Colonial architectural styles have always been my favorite, but unfortunately I have never been able to buy a colonial house. Would there be any problem in adding a colonial-style broken pediment over the front door of my current house, which is a rough-stone row house built about 1890?

Putting a colonial pediment on your 1890 house would be like painting over your grandfather's portrait, blotting out his handlebar mustache and giving him a peruke. Alterations to a historic building should never attempt to create a style earlier than that of the original building.

My partner and I have recently purchased a late 19th-century bakery that we plan to renovate for use as a pizza parlor. The building has a number of interesting wood-frame, multipane windows that, unfortunately, need repair. The contractor has insisted on replacing all the windows with single-pane fixed glass, but I hesitate to remove the original windows. Do you have any suggestions?

The decision to repair or replace windows is an issue that can pose considerable problems in rehabilitating historic commercial structures. If a small number of undistinguished windows on secondary elevations are deteriorated, then total replacement of these windows may be an appropriate avenue to pursue. Stock windows are often adequate replacements because of their availability, low cost and energy efficiency.

Certain historic structures, such as your building, may have highly distinctive windows that are a major component of the overall exterior design. In this case, the distinguishing original features should not be destroyed, and careful repair of the deteriorated elements is the preferred approach. In the event that repair is not technically or economically feasible, new windows could be substituted for missing or irreparable windows; these should match the original in material, size, general muntin and mullion configuration and reflective qualities of the glass.

My 1930s brick laundry and dry-cleaning plant has three-part steel awning windows. The top two panes of glass are fixed, but the bottom one opens out. I like the appearance of these old windows, but they are drafty and some sections are rusting. I would like to replace the windows with ones of better quality, but my employees like the natural ventilation that the open-out windows provide during spring and summer. What should I do?

Repair and upgrade the windows. First, remove rust with a wire brush, and then prime and paint the frames with a high-quality, corrosion-resistant exterior oil paint specifically intended for steel windows. Installing weatherstripping will greatly reduce drafts and therefore improve thermal efficiency. Second, to improve thermal efficiency even more, you might consider installing triple-track, double-hung, aluminum frame storm windows on the interior. The meeting rail could be at the base of the two fixed panes of glass, leaving you with a large, fixed upper sash and a small, lower operable sash with a screen. This type of storm window would not visually detract from the window's exterior appearance but would allow the existing awning window to be operable, thus allowing ventilation during spring and summer as well as providing the added thermal benefit of a second layer of glazing during the colder months. However, there is a risk of condensation causing rust on the inside of the steel awning window. If condensation occurs, simply wipe up the moisture periodically before it causes a problem.

Because of the rising cost of heating a house, our local historic district review board may revise the district's design guidelines to allow storm doors on front entrances of houses. The residents of the district are divided on the subject. Can you give us some advice on the appropriateness of this change?

Storm doors can make a house more comfortable in the winter by reducing heat lost through conduction and air infiltration around the door and by controlling drafts when the door is opened. However, storm doors are often not cost effective—that is, not enough money is saved from reduced energy bills to equal the cost of the storm door. Storm doors are most cost effective when the house is located in the colder regions of the country and when the door opens directly into the living area. For moderately cold climates, storm doors are not generally considered cost effective unless the primary door is hollow-core or is more than 25 percent glass. Your local utility company or state energy office should be able to advise you further and to suggest other efficient and cost-effective measures for conserving energy for your house, taking into account the climate of your particular region.

If the house owners and review board decide that storm doors will be effective in saving energy and utility costs, keep the following facts in mind. Proper installation and weatherstripping will improve a storm door's thermal performance. The more glass a storm door has, the less effective it is as insulation. Storm doors with pseudotraditional design elements such as scallops, eagles or other insignia should be avoided in favor of simple, unobtrusive, contemporary designs that do not obscure the historic door. Storm doors also should be painted a color compatible with that of the front door and the house; aluminum doors should also be painted.

The wooden windowsills in our church are rotting in places. A member of our congregation suggests covering the sills with thin aluminum sheeting that can be easily cut to fit the existing sill, nailed down and painted to match the rest of the building. He also says that this application will prevent the wood from rotting further because it will keep water from collecting on the sill. I have heard that aluminum siding should not be used on historic frame buildings, but would this limited application be acceptable?

No. Such a solution would not be acceptable, because aluminum would only cover up the problem instead of correcting it. As you have already discovered, horizontal exterior wood surfaces are vulnerable to moisture deterioration. However, if you simply cover the damaged sills, fungi (one type is dry rot) will continue to grow and, if left unchecked, will spread to other portions of the church.

The best method for repairing rotten wooden windowsills is to dry the wood, treat it with a fungicide and then use an epoxy patching compound to strengthen, consolidate and build up the sill. After the epoxy has dried, the sill can be sanded, primed and painted with an enamel-finish paint.

If the sills are badly decayed and beyond repair, you may have to replace them with new wooden ones. However, this procedure can be very complicated, because the sills are tied into the building's framing. If replacement is the only reasonable solution, cut the new wood to match the original sills in proportion and detail. Then treat the exposed areas with a wood preservative. (If a preservative containing pentachlorophenol is used, extreme care should be taken because of the chemical's toxicity.) Set the new sills so that they slope slightly away from the window, thus allowing rain and melting snow to drain off. Caulk areas where the sill meets the window frame and the siding. Finally, prime the new sill and paint with a high-quality exterior paint.

I am considering adding an awning over the window of my shop, which was constructed at the turn of the century. What are the guidelines for installing awnings? The building is in a local historic district.

When based on historical precedent, canvas awnings can be an attractive addition to older commercial buildings. Awnings can help shelter passersby, reduce glare and conserve energy by controlling the amount of sunlight hitting the windows. In many cases, awnings can disguise inappropriate alterations to a facade that may be too expensive to remove; they can also provide additional color as well as a strong commercial identification. Fixed aluminum awnings and awnings simulating mansard roofs and umbrellas are generally inappropriate for older commercial buildings. If you add awnings, choose a style made from soft canvas or nonshiny vinyl materials; be certain that they are installed without damaging the building or visually impairing distinctive architectural features. To achieve maximum energy conservation, awnings should also be operable.

We plan a new living-room addition to the rear of our Federal-style house, which is located in a historic district. This work must be approved by our local design review board, but before I discuss it with the members, I want to know whether moving the front door closer to the addition and replacing it with a bay window is likely to be approved.

If the board members do not reject the plan, they should. Even without seeing a photograph of your house or district or a sketch of the plans for the addition, we can provide some general advice. Doors on front facades are important architectural features that often display distinguishing stylistic elements and are usually an integral part of the overall design of a building's facade. Removing the original door and replacing it with a window that did not exist historically can seriously damage the character of your historic house. Rather than remove the historic door, you should retain it and include a door on the new addition.

Additions to historic houses should be located on secondary or rear facades (where you have indicated yours will be) and should be compatible in scale, size, materials and color with the original house. However, the design of the new addition should not attempt to replicate the style of the original house. Building additions and alterations should not seek to imitate an earlier style or period. Also, additions should be constructed so that any damage to historic fabric is minimal and that the new construction could be removed at a later date, leaving the original form and integrity of the historic house intact.

The tower of our turreted Queen Anne-style house has a double-hung window, the top pane of which is still filled with highly decorative stained glass. The bottom pane has been replaced with clear glass. How would I go about replacing the plain glass to match the original?

One recent and encouraging development is the growing number of craftsmen working in stained and beveled glass. If you can afford to have a window made, you should have no great difficulty finding someone to duplicate the original pattern. Otherwise, you may be able to find a close match for the existing window from an architectural salvage firm.

It would be advisable, however, to leave the plain window as it is rather than replace it with a stained-glass window that differs noticeably from the original.

We live in a row house in a large midwestern city. The front door opens directly onto the living area. We are considering installing an exterior vestibule to cut down on energy losses. What do you think of this idea?

The most effective and often the most cost-efficient ways to save energy inside the house are (1) decreasing the occupants' energy use; (2) tightening the building envelope with insulation, weatherstripping and caulking; (3) using thermal shutters, curtains or storm windows to decrease heat loss in winter and heat gain in summer; and (4) ensuring that the mechanical systems are in good operating condition. More efficient furnaces, hot-water heaters and major appliances are being developed every year. If a furnace is more than 15 years old, an owner should consider replacing it.

Before making any costly energy conservation improvements, such as constructing an exterior vestibule, have your house audited to determine where major energy losses are occurring. A good audit should include an on-site analysis by a professional of the house's exterior envelope and areas of infiltration, utility bills and occupants' habits and an examination of the mechanical systems. Utility companies, private consultants and building contractors perform audits at varying levels of cost and thoroughness. If your energy audit determines that you have taken all the measures suggested here, other energy conservation measures are probably not essential.

Vestibules prevent air infiltration when the front door is opened. However, constructing the vestibule would probably not be cost effective; the energy savings would be small compared to the construction costs. In addition, the vestibule may have a negative effect on your house's historic facade and your streetscape. However, if you want to cut down on drafts to make the room more comfortable rather than to save money on energy bills, try an appropriately designed storm door. An interior vestibule is another alternative, but it would be costly and would absorb part of your living room space. An interior vestibule should not be considered if its construction would irreversibly alter significant historic fabric or spaces.

To save energy this winter I plan to turn off the heat in several upstairs rooms at the front of our row house. I also plan to board up the windows to be doubly sure that no heat escapes. I realize that boarded-up windows may not look attractive, but isn't saving energy more important than saving appearances?

You should focus your energy conservation efforts on reducing air infiltration between these rooms and the heated portions of the house. Boarding up windows not only looks unsightly but also could make your house appear vacant, thus possibly encouraging burglaries.

Weatherstrip around the doors to these rooms and caulk all cracks on the interior walls that abut the unheated rooms. These cracks are usually found around door frames and where baseboards and cornices meet the floor and ceiling. Also caulk around pipes and ducts entering these walls. Use Underwriters Laboratories—approved foam gaskets behind wall sockets on these walls.

If the unheated rooms include a bathroom or if water pipes run through the walls or floors of the unheated rooms, you will have to take some extra precautions. Water in unused systems, such as bathroom fixtures, pipes and radiators, should be drained to avoid freezing. You should also check where water pipes serving the rest of the house run before cutting off the heat in these rooms. If the pipes are located within exterior walls and are uninsulated, they may freeze during the winter. If you live in a severe climate, you should probably not consider this method of energy conservation unless you are certain that no water will be carried through these unheated areas.

I own a brick commercial building dating from 1883. The storefronts, which were altered in the 1930s, have now rusted beyond repair. Should I try to replicate the 1930s storefront design, which is quite attractive, or go back to the late 19th-century look?

You are fortunate to have several options in your rehabilitation planning, but retaining the building's commercial appearance should be the major consideration. First, you may want to replicate the 1930s storefronts if their design is compatible with the building's original architectural features. Second, new storefronts could be designed that are clearly contemporary but that are compatible with the scale, design, materials, color and texture of the building. (Introducing a recessed arcade or other radically different design element, for example, would probably not be in keeping with your own building or your neighbors' and thus should be avoided. Similarly, contemporary treatments that substitute masonry for glass are also likely to be inappropriate.) Finally, if pictorial or physical evidence is found that documents the original configuration of the ground floor, an accurate restoration could be undertaken.

I own a late 19th-century Victorian commercial building. The original storefront was replaced in the 1950s with one that is incompatible with the rest of the building. How should I proceed to give the front a more compatible look?

Without knowing more about the building than your question relates, it is impossible to give specific advice on how to rehabilitate the storefront. However, the following general principles apply to any rehabilitation effort.

Determine the style of your building and how the storefront was intended to complement the entire facade. Do not "antique" a front; avoid stock "lumberyard colonial" detailing such as coach lanterns, mansard overhangings, wood shakes, nonoperable shutters and small-paned windows unless they were used historically. Preserve the storefront character of the building even though the structure may serve a different use at present. If less exposed window area is desirable, consider using interior blinds and curtains rather than altering the existing historic fabric. Avoid using materials that were unavailable when the building was constructed, such as vinyl and aluminum siding, anodized aluminum, tinted glass, artificial stone and brick veneer. Choose paint colors based on the building's historical appearance. Do not coat surfaces that have never been painted. For 19th-century storefronts, two contrasting colors may be appropriate, but if you use more than two you run the risk of giving the building an inappropriate appearance.

ALTERED STOREFRONTS

I have just renovated my store, which is in the middle of my town's historic district, and want a new sign as a final touch. What are the guidelines for the use of signs?

Signs were an integral component of 19th- and 20th-century storefronts and today play an important role in defining the character of a business district. Photographs of historic streetscapes reveal a multitude of signs—in windows, over doors, painted on exterior walls and hanging over (and sometimes across) the street. Although this confusion was part of the character of 19th-century cities and towns, today's approach towards signs in historic districts tends to be much more conservative.

Removal of modern backlit fluorescent signs, large applied signs with distinctive corporate logos and other signs attached to the building that obscure significant architectural detailing can dramatically improve the visual appearance of a building; for this reason, removal of these signs is encouraged in the process of rehabilitation. If new signs are designed, their size and style should be compatible with the historic building and should not cover or obscure significant architectural detailing. During the 19th century, signs for buildings were commonly mounted on the lintel at the top of the first story. Another common approach, especially at the turn of the century, was to paint signs directly on the inside of the display windows; frequently these were painted in gold leaf. New hanging signs may be appropriate for historic commercial buildings if their scale and design are compatible with the historic building. Signs and advertising painted on exterior walls should be retained if they have historical or artistic significance, especially if they provide evidence of early or original occupants.

Our department store has beautiful bronze frames around the windows, but they have been painted over the years. How can we restore their original appearance?

Bronze storefronts, common to large commercial buildings and major department stores during the 20th century, can be cleaned by a variety of methods. Excessive cleaning may remove some surface metal or patina, however, and should be attempted only when encrusted salts, paint, bird droppings or dirt must be removed.

Fine glass-bead blasting (or peening) and crushed walnut shell blasting are acceptable mechanical methods if carried out in controlled circumstances under low pressure (80–100 pounds per square inch). All adjacent wood or masonry should be protected from the blasting. Chemical compounds such as rottenstone and oil, whiting and ammonia, or precipitated chalk and ammonia can be rubbed onto bronze surfaces with little or no damage. A compound used successfully by a number of commercial cleaning companies has a base solution of 5 percent oxalic acid and water, which is then mixed with finely ground India pumice powder.

The 1890s two-story commercial building that I now own has a tacky storefront that was added sometime in the 1940s, presumably to "modernize" the building. I want to know what is underneath the storefront, but so far I have been unable to find any pictures of the earlier front. How can I find out whether the original storefront still exists without taking the expensive gamble of ripping down the present one?

If the present storefront is a relatively recent addition with little or no architectural merit, begin by removing a few inconspicuous parts of the covering materials. Storefronts of the 1940s and 1950s were installed frequently by attaching studs or a metal grid over an early front and applying new covering materials. Pry away the covering pieces in several places to determine the materials underneath. Be sure to check several different locations because important elements may have been damaged or destroyed in the process of installing the later front. If this preliminary investigation reveals evidence of an earlier front, carefully remove the later material to assess the overall condition of the historic storefront. In many cases the modern coverings were nailed directly into the original facade. Removing such fronts, therefore, will almost certainly create holes that will need repair. Be prepared also to discover that projecting pilasters, cornices and other ornamental features may have been broken off to make flat surfaces on which to attach the later front; these will need repair or replacement.

I own a small commercial building that was constructed about 1935. The area beneath the first-floor storefront windows is decorated with panels of what appears to be colored glass. One of these panels has been broken and replaced at some time with a substitute material. Is it possible to find a more suitable replacement?

The panels to which you refer are most likely a material called pigmented structural glass, although it was not really structural but merely served as a decorative facing material. It was used primarily on shopfronts and restaurants from slightly after the turn of the century until about 1950. Three companies manufactured this glass, and each had its own trademarked name—Marietta Manufacturing Company produced Sani Onyx, Libbey-Owens-Ford produced Vitrolite and Pittsburgh Plate Glass produced Carrara Glass. This glass came in a wide range of colors, thicknesses and finishes, although the smooth, mirrorlike surface was probably the most popular. The glass panels were easily attached to the wall surface with an asphaltic mastic, with further support provided by shelf angles.

Both Libbey-Owens-Ford and Pittsburgh Plate Glass today make similar products—Vitrolux (LOF) and Spandrelite (PPG); unfortunately, they are not good replacements because their composition and colors differ considerably from the original materials. To replace the glass, therefore, try to find salvaged Carrara Glass or Vitrolite that is undamaged and that matches the missing piece. If that option is not feasible, it may be possible to replace missing or damaged glass in a prominent place on the facade with undamaged glass from an inconspicuous place.

A 1910 church in our community that has not been used for several years has been purchased by a developer who plans to rehabilitate it for use as a two-story office with an English basement. Although I am pleased that the building will not be demolished, I am concerned about the developer's intention to remove the original, highly ornate front entrance—including doors, steps and railings—to provide easier access for clients. A parking lot is to be built adjacent to the church. Are there any design solutions that might allow the front entrance to be saved, such as using the side entrance?

Lowering the main entrance steps will not change the number of levels within the church, so the developer must be planning to put in an elevator. Suggest that he investigate the possibility of constructing stairs or a ramp at the side entrance closest to the parking lot down half a level to an attractive lower-level lobby that would connect with the main elevator. This approach would preserve the ceremonial front entrance, which is obviously an integral part of the character of the historic property. With careful planning, both the front and side entrances could be used, with a directory of offices posted on each level.

We are renovating an 80-year-old house. The wooden porch is in good structural condition, but the paint has almost completely peeled off the flooring, and the tongue-and-groove pine boards appear dried out. A few areas need minor patching, but not enough deterioration is present to warrant replacing boards. What should we do to preserve the porch?

After you have scraped and sanded the porch to remove any remaining blistered paint and to smooth all rough edges, follow this four-step procedure: (1) Treat the wood with a coat of penetrating water-repellent preservative; (2) fill any holes with a wood filler and sand smooth; (3) apply a coat of high-quality exterior oil primer; and (4) apply one or more coats of matching porch and deck enamel.

Applying the water-repellent preservative is a very important step. The preservative contains a penetrating oil, which revitalizes the wood, as well as a fungicide, which retards mildew growth and insect infestation. It also acts as a water repellent, reducing warping and staining of the board ends. The solution is applied by brushing or spraying; all surfaces and edges should be liberally treated. Because of the toxicity of these preservatives, be very careful to avoid coming in contact with them and breathing the vapors. Shrubs and plants also should be protected from contamination. Of the two types of fungicides generally available, copper and zinc napthanate is less dangerous than pentachlorophenol. To avoid intercoat peeling and blistering, the applied paint should not be exposed to full sun or evening dew (common during the spring and fall) for the first two days. Also, allow no more than two weeks' drying time between coats.

I rent a townhouse in a historic downtown area. A main feature of the houses on my block is their decorative cast-iron front steps. My landlord, who is generally conscientious about making repairs, is threatening to remove the railings because he claims they are wobbly and could cause an accident. Please tell me whether a wobbly cast-iron railing is repairable. The iron is not cracked anywhere.

Removing or replacing the railings is probably unnecessary and could also alter the historical cohesiveness of your block. A wobbling rail or other loose cast-iron element can usually be corrected by tightening all bolts and screws (most architectural cast iron is made up of many small castings originally painted with a prime coat and assembled by bolts or screws). If tightening the bolts does not solve the problem, the threads are probably stripped or the bolts rusted; the next logical step is to replace the old bolts and screws with new ones. Sometimes increasing the diameter of the bolt or screw is necessary to compensate for loss of metal around it caused by rusting.

I am a member of a historical society that has been holding its meetings in a magnificent late 19th-century Classical Revival mansion for the past 15 years. Now part of the building is to be converted to office space, and a two-story porch, located at the rear of the building, is being enclosed to provide an additional conference room. We are worried that this plan to enclose the porch will ruin this prominent feature of the building.

If the porch is enclosed with glass rather than a solid material, the plan may be successful, but, even if glass is used, great care must be taken to retain the form and integrity of the porch. Two important points should be raised when discussing the rehabilitation plan with the owner and project architect: (1) The large glass walls should be placed behind the porch columns and balusters, with most of the framing members and meeting rails hidden behind the columns and balusters, and (2) none of the columns or balusters should be removed during the alteration. Enclosing a porch is an acceptable preservation practice if historic materials are retained and the newly enclosed space still gives the appearance of a porch.

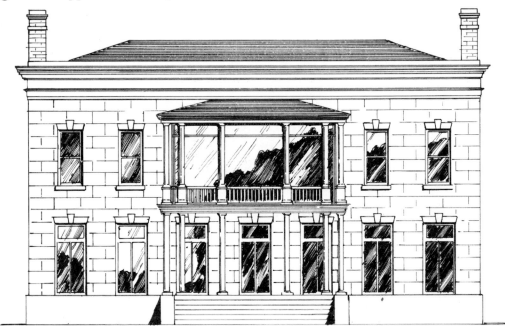

We have just purchased an early 20th-century Boston townhouse and were surprised to discover that the deteriorated balusters on the parapet and balcony rails were terra cotta instead of stone. Is there any way to replace the damaged and missing balusters?

Glazed architectural terra cotta was a popular ornamental masonry material in America from the late 19th century through the 1930s. Relatively inexpensive, it was widely used to imitate stone for window and door surrounds, belt-courses, balustrades and entablatures.

Your missing balusters may be replaced with new terra cotta or a substitute material. Terra cotta is still being manufactured in the United States, but only on a limited basis. The delivery time is often lengthy and the cost prohibitive. As an alternative you could use precast tinted concrete with lightweight aggregate that matches the existing undamaged balusters in form, color and finish. Many manufacturers of precast concrete items such as urns and garden statues (often called cast stone) can make satisfactory reproductions for missing terra-cotta pieces.

Carefully remove an undamaged baluster for use in creating a mold. The replacement baluster may be coated with a clear or tinted masonry coating to approximate the reflectivity of the original finish and protect it from water damage.

Remember to demand high-quality reproduction work; the replacement pieces should be undetectable from the original. It is also important to use an experienced mason. Terra-cotta detailing is a complex assembling of many small interconnected pieces; it is never the province of do-it-yourselfers.

Other substitute materials include cast fiber glass and natural stone. However, precast concrete is the most satisfactory, inexpensive and expedient substitute material.

I am making wooden balusters to repair the damaged ones on my front porch. Rather than use chemical preservatives, I want to use wood that is naturally resistant to decay and termite damage. What kind of wood should I use?

Natural toxic substances deposited in the cell structure of certain species of wood make the heartwood resistant to decay or termite attack. Decay-resistant species include bald cypress, cedar, redwood, black locust and black walnut. Termite-resistant species include bald cypress, redwood and eastern red cedar. Your decision will probably be based to a large extent on the availability of such wood types in your area.

I have moved into a clapboard and shingle house that dates from the 1880s. The previous owners removed all the old paint because they said it was in terrible condition. The clapboards are now painted a soft brown, with the trim a light yellow and sash and shutters a somewhat darker yellow. The shingles have been coated with a brown stain. I am just beginning to research colors appropriate to the neighborhood in the late 19th century. Are the existing colors generally on target?

It is a shame that the previous owners did not think to leave a record of the paint layers for future investigators, but, because they did not, your research into neighborhood colors is a good preservation approach.

The color of your house at present would seem appropriate, with the possible exception of the sash and shutters, which generally should be the darkest parts of the house. According to Roger Moss in *Century of Color*, "Especially on houses erected between 1840 and 1900, the sash will be darker than the trim, usually deep reddish or chocolate brown, dark green, olive, or even black. This gives the effect of the windows receding into the facade rather than projecting, which is exactly the effect that was intended." As to the shutters, he continues, "Often they are painted in the trim color with recessed panels picked out in the body color, or in an even darker shade of the body-trim combination."

The paint on the exterior wooden decorative trim of my 1880s brick townhouse is chalking. My contractor suggests removing all the paint and varnishing the exposed wood. Is this type of treatment recommended?

No. Many people believe that the exterior wooden portions of historic buildings were never painted, but most were, especially those of a house like the one you have described. If you follow your contractor's advice, you will be creating a new appearance for your house, not restoring it.

Also, varnish is not as durable as paint. The sun's ultraviolet rays tend to break down a clear varnish faster than an opaque paint. An opaque stain with a sun block is more durable, but paint will last far longer.

We recently bought an old house that is in good condition, except that the top layer of paint on the eaves is peeling. What caused this problem, and how can we correct it?

This condition is known as intercoat peeling and is generally caused by improper surface preparation or incompatibility of paints. Eaves, covered porches or other protected areas are not rinsed by the rain, so salts or impurities from previous layers of paint accumulate on the surface. New paint will not adhere properly if these impurities are not cleaned off. Intercoat peeling could also occur if latex paint is applied over old oil paint before an oil primer is applied.

It will probably be difficult to tell which condition caused your problem, so scrape all loose paint down to the next sound layer. Then thoroughly wash the surface with a strong stream of water, wipe dry, sand by hand and repaint with a high-quality exterior oil paint.

The exterior paint below the windows of my 1920 house is covered with mold or mildew. Should I sand it off before repainting?

No. Sanding will not kill fungal growth. Using the following solution, scrub with a medium-hard natural-bristle brush until the growth is bleached white: 3 ounces trisodium phosphate, l ounce detergent, 1 quart 5 percent hypochlorite bleach and 3 quarts warm water. Wash away the solution with a garden hose, allow the surface to dry thoroughly and then sand by hand and apply a mildew-resistant paint. Because moisture probably caused the mildew or mold, you should try to locate and eliminate its source so that such growth will not recur and lead to more serious problems.

The paint on my porch railing is so seriously cracked that I am afraid it will have to be removed completely before the porch can be repainted. The painting contractor assures me that using a blowtorch is the quickest method of removing paint. Are there dangers in using this method?

Blowtorches, such as hand-held propane or butane torches, were widely used for removing paint before other thermal devices became available. However, removing paint with the use of a blowtorch can be extremely dangerous; both the heat gun and the heat plate are generally safer to use.

With a blowtorch, the flame is directed toward the paint until it begins to bubble and loosen from the surface. Then the paint is scraped off with a putty knife. Although this process is relatively quick, the open flame, which can reach temperatures between 3,200 and 3,800 degrees Fahrenheit, can burn a careless operator and cause severe damage to eyes and skin; it also can easily scorch or ignite the wood, or even burn down a building. Another fire hazard is more insidious. Most frame buildings have an air space between the exterior sheathing and siding and the interior lath and plaster. This cavity usually has an accumulation of dust, which could also be easily ignited by the open flame of a blowtorch. A further danger: The lead in old paints will vaporize at high temperatures, releasing toxic fumes that can be unknowingly inhaled. For all these reasons, the blowtorch should definitely be avoided.

The original carving on the wooden brackets of the porch of my 1880s Italianate house is hidden under layers of paint. Should I remove all the paint or leave well enough alone?

Opinion varies as to whether heavy paint buildup justifies removing layers of paint. Generally, if there are no signs of paint failure, such as cracking, peeling or "alligatoring," the surface should be left alone. The paint is a partial record of the building's evolution, but, even more important, it protects the wood. If, at a later time, signs of paint failure appear, the damaged paint should be removed by scraping and sanding to the next sound layer and the wood repainted. If, however, paint failure has reached the bare wood, total paint removal is justified, either with a heat gun (one that heats to 500 to 750 degrees Fahrenheit) or with chemical strippers. Both methods require laborious manual scraping. Detachable wooden elements, such as exterior shutters, may be sent out for commercial dipping, but the company's work should be seen before a decision is made.

The wood siding on the outside of my 1920s house needs repainting. How can I find out whether lead paints were ever used? If they were used, what is the safest way to remove them?

Because your house was constructed before 1950, it is more than likely that lead paint was used. To test for lead paint, ask your pharmacist to prepare a 5 percent sodium sulfide solution. Then clean a small area of the siding. Scratch the paint, exposing the previous layers, and apply a drop of the solution. If the solution turns gray to black within 90 seconds, lead paint is present. Dispose of the sodium sulfide carefully because it is poisonous.

The easiest and safest way to remove lead paint is with an electric heat plate. It operates at temperatures of 550 to 800 degrees Fahrenheit and softens the paint enough so you can scrape it off. Follow these safety precautions: Avoid contact with the element; keep a fire extinguisher close by; wear protective goggles; use the heat plate only in dry weather and with heavy-duty extension cords; wash yourself and your clothes afterwards and be very careful when disposing of the scrapings.

I am planning to restore the interior of my post-Civil War house, and I have discovered a historic photograph of the front parlor that shows the furniture, curtains and rugs. Can I use this photograph as a guide in my restoration, or were such photographs frequently staged?

The majority of photographs from this period were taken by photographers who were interested primarily in documenting a room as it actually appeared, although they may have added a few additional palms or other insignificant decorative items. Even with these props, however, the essential character of the interior would hardly be affected.

In your attempt to re-create the desired period, bear in mind that middle-class American homes, unlike mansions of the wealthy, usually reflected a mixture of styles.

We have just purchased a 1910 bank building in a small nearby town that we plan to use as the location for one of our branch banks. Unfortunately, long before we purchased the building, the interior of the first-floor banking room was gutted, leaving what is now a generously proportioned but basically characterless interior space. Photographs in our possession document the original interior. We want our rehabilitation for office space to be sympathetic to the Classical Revival style of the building. How should we proceed?

Because the building has been completely divested of its original interiors, you do not have to be concerned about saving original historic fabric and you have some latitude in choosing how to rehabilitate the interior. Therefore, you may choose either a contemporary or a historical treatment. Because you are fortunate enough to have photographs of the original interior and because the intended reuse is the same as the original use, you should make an effort to duplicate the most significant of the original features, such as the tellers' counters, the customers' check-writing counters, any important lighting fixtures, decorative hardwood, woodwork and perhaps even the vault. All this duplication probably will be quite expensive, of course; consequently, you might want to consider replicating only a few of the more noteworthy features of the original banking room interior. Selected duplicated historical features could be attractively blended within a traditional interior framework featuring simple wood moldings, doors and window frames. An alternative would be to remodel the banking room in a clearly contemporary style.

All these options would be acceptable treatments for an interior of a historic building that has lost its original or period features. The one approach not recommended, and which would not be acceptable, is to re-create a period interior not representative of the historical style of the building.

The plaster ceiling of my old house is peeling and badly patched. It also has a few minor cracks. Are there any quick repair methods that do not require a professional plasterer?

There are several methods of covering damaged plaster ceilings with substitute materials, but none is quick. These alternatives also are not suitable for ceilings decorated with raised plaster because the decoration would be destroyed in the process. But for plain plastered ceilings that you do not wish to replaster and repaint, one historic method still valid today is to apply wallpaper or fabric over the entire ceiling. More modern methods involve fiber-glass sheeting and special adhesives. Application procedures here, however, are more complex than traditional wallpaper or fabric applications. Moreover, because these products are fairly new, their long-term effects on paint and plaster as well as their bonding capabilities are less certain.

The plaster walls in my house are bulging and cracking in several places. How can they be repaired?

Bulging or loose plaster is caused when the lathing pulls away from the supporting studs or when the plaster pulls loose from the lath. The first condition is less serious. To determine what has caused the bulging, break through the plaster in one or two small areas. If the lath has pulled loose from the studs, break out more plaster so that all the loose lath is exposed. Then reattach the lath with screws and washers.

If the key (the bond between the plaster and the lath) has been broken, simply remove the loose plaster and replaster. But if the original plaster must be retained, your repairs are going to be more complex, time-consuming and expensive, perhaps necessitating professional advice.

First, try using fasteners with washers, screwing or nailing the plaster to the lath. Place such anchors at 8- to 12-inch intervals across the face of the loose plaster. Countersink the fasteners and then replaster.

If the plaster can be reached from behind, use a plywood brace to bring the loose plaster back to its original position. Then apply fresh plaster to the back of the existing plaster to re-establish a key. If any lath is missing, you can nail in some new wire lath, rock lath or plasterboard.

A final method involves injecting into the plaster a commercial liquid adhesive that contains a bonding agent, lime and a lightweight aggregate. Immediately after the injection, place a plywood brace against the plaster to bring it back to its original position while the adhesive cures. You may have to repeat this procedure several times until the adhesive holds.

We recently had the dining room of our 1885 townhouse professionally replastered, and then we painted the plaster ourselves with oil primer and finish coats. Now, much to our dismay, the surface is discolored and blistering. What caused this reaction?

You did not mention how long the plaster was allowed to dry after it had been applied, but you may not have waited long enough. Fresh plaster (as well as fresh concrete, mortar and stucco) must be permitted to cure before it is painted. If the building temperature is above 50 degrees Fahrenheit and the relative humidity below 70 percent, three to four weeks is generally sufficient drying time. If the surface has to be painted before curing, a good latex primer can probably be applied successfully. Because latex is water-permeable, moisture from the drying plaster is able to escape. When you applied an oil paint, which is far less permeable, over your uncured plaster, the evaporating moisture caused the surface to blister. You should scrape and sand all affected areas, wait until you are certain the plaster has cured and then apply a high-quality oil finish coat, which should adhere.

Underneath some fairly shabby linoleum in my kitchen is a handsome hardwood floor. What is the easiest way to take up the old linoleum?

Starting in a corner of the kitchen, pry up the edge of the linoleum with a chisel and gently chip through the adhesive beneath the tile. The sticky substance that remains on the floor can be softened with a solvent such as turpentine or mineral spirits and then scraped off by hand with a putty knife or wide scraper. Although this process will probably be long and physically exhausting, it is preferable to sanding off the glue with a power sander because the glue coats the sanding disk so quickly that you spend more time changing the sandpaper than actually removing the glue.

I have a badly worn historic linoleum floor in my old house. Should I try to repair it or simply replace it?

Linoleum, the floor covering made of a linseed oil cement pressed onto burlap or other fabric, was invented by Frederick Walton, who built the first factory for its manufacture in Staines, England, in 1864. The cement was composed of oxidized linseed oil, rosin and pigments and, more recently, oxidized linseed oil, wood flour (or cork), ground limestone and pigments. Because linoleum can withstand contact with oils and fats, changes in temperature and aging, it saw increased production until the late 1940s, when its popularity declined in favor of vinyl and other synthetic floorings. Manufacture of linoleum was discontinued in the United States about six years ago.

Although linoleum is quite durable, when exposed to moisture and alkaline conditions it slowly deteriorates; therefore, it is not a suitable covering for damp cement floors. Only mild detergents, not strong detergents or solvents, should be used to clean it. Questions concerning its care can be directed to the Armstrong Cork Company, Liberty and Charlotte streets, Lancaster, Pa. 17604.

For replacement or reproduction, two European firms still manufacture a linoleum line: Krommenie in Holland (contact: Kiefer International Products, 219 Michigan Street, N.E., Grand Rapids, Mich. 49503) and Barry Staines in England (contact: Dodge Corporation, Laurel and Manor streets, Lancaster, Pa. 17603).

Our house has several painted wooden doors and mantels that I would like to strip to bare wood. Would the wood be damaged if it were commercially dipped in a lye or caustic bath to remove the paint?

The effect of this treatment varies, depending both on the type of wood and how carefully the work is done. Although dipping softwoods and oak in lye is usually acceptable if done quickly and carefully, walnut and other hardwoods should not be dipped in lye because dipping darkens the wood. Although hardwood can be lightened later with bleach, bleaching may destroy the appearance of the wood, a change that would be particularly noticeable if the wood were refinished with a traditional varnish coating.

First, find out whether your pieces are made of softwood or hardwood. Then, before contracting to have large pieces dipped, take a small, insignificant piece to be dipped. If you are satisfied with the results, have your doors and mantels dipped. Dipping has the effect of raising the grain of the wood, and some wood that has been dipped comes out looking like shredded wheat. To reduce the risk of damage, talk to people who have had wood dipped by firms in your area. Ask to see the piece that was dipped; what one person thinks is a good job may not satisfy you. Finally, always take the work to the company in the morning and pick it up in the afternoon; some companies do the easy work during the day and let the difficult jobs soak overnight.

The kitchen in my house, which dates from 1903, has a tin ceiling covered with many layers of paint. How can I get rid of the paint easily, touch up rust spots and protect the ceiling after the paint has been removed?

First, you should give up the idea of removing the paint and, instead, accustom yourself to having a painted ceiling. Removing paint from a ceiling can be quite difficult and dangerous. Repainting is the easiest and, thus, the most logical way to approach this problem; it can be done after sanding lightly by hand to remove any rust spots or chipping paint.

If, however, you are still determined to remove the paint, you may wish to use a chemical paint stripper, applying it with a brush. Be very careful to keep it out of your eyes and off your skin, as most chemical paint removers are caustic. In this instance, it is not safe to use a heat gun to assist in removing paint because of the high risk of igniting flammable material on or above the ceiling. If you are successful in removing the paint completely, you can eliminate any rust spots by sanding lightly; the bare metal ceiling can then be coated with a clear lacquer.

Our 1906 house has decorative cast-iron radiators with an embossed curvilinear floral pattern at the top and bottom. Should the embossed pattern be painted a contrasting color? We want to treat the radiators authentically.

Yes, ornamental radiators were often painted in two colors, usually repeating the colors of the wallpaper. A 1905 catalog of the American Radiator Company describes several decorative schemes using contrasting colors—for instance, a moss green background with the embossed area highlighted with creamy yellow, a rust red background with beige highlights, and a lemon yellow background with white highlights.

The manufacturer's recommendation for painting the radiators with enamel paint is this: First, paint the entire radiator with the highlight color and let it dry completely. Then paint the entire radiator with the background color, letting it dry only to the tacky stage. Then take a clean cloth and rub the embossed area, removing the background color and leaving the highlighted color to show through.

This approach is easier than trying to paint the embossed area by hand. The radiators should be painted when cold, and the heat should not be turned on for at least 24 hours after painting.

I want to remove the plastic brick that covers my kitchen walls. How can I do this without damaging the wall underneath?

Plastic brick and other types of veneer products, such as simulated stone and wood paneling, are promoted strictly for cosmetic purposes and are installed either with tacks or adhesive. If tacks were used, simply remove each tack and then patch the holes.

If an adhesive was used, first pry off the bricks with a screwdriver or other chisellike tool. Then try one of the following treatments to remove the dried adhesive from the wall. Because various manufacturers use different adhesives, first test a small area to determine which method works best.

Your first option is simple scraping, which may prove ineffective because of the hardness of the glue.

A second option is to soften the adhesive using heat. Some adhesives have very high melting points and can be softened by a direct flame (a butane torch, for instance). But because of the flammability of the adhesive and the likelihood of toxic fumes, use a hot air gun.

A third option is to use a chemical paint stripper. Chemicals will soften the adhesive, but they should be used only in a well-ventilated area, away from sparks and fires.

If none of these methods works, you may want to remove the affected portion of the wall and install a new surface, such as plasterboard. However, this option may be unacceptable if the new surface obscures door or window frames or trim, baseboards and cornices.

The historic house where I serve as docent has a number of slate fireplaces, but some have lost their marbleized enameling. We know little about the history of this type of decorative painting. Can you shed some light on this subject?

Marbleizing has been practiced since Roman times. It was popular in the United States during the 19th century and grew into a prominent industry in the 1870s, when mantels, fireboards, columns, furniture elements and even coffins were marbleized. There are several methods of marbleizing, one of the most common of which is a painting process similar to artificial graining.

In the marbleizing process the slate was rubbed with pumice so that the oil colors would adhere to the surface; it was then polished with pulverized pumice and felt and painted with a background color. The slate was dipped in a vat containing water on which the oil paint had been sprinkled and then stirred or fanned with a brush to give a variegated, marbleized appearance. The process ended with a series of bakings and polishings. A coat of varnish often was applied as a last step. Various types of marble could be imitated by using different colors.

How can paint be removed from fireplace brick?

This task is a difficult one and is not always successful. Most fireplace bricks were painted after they had become blackened with soot, so be prepared for dirty bricks beneath the paint. If the bricks are rough textured with vertical grooves, it may be impossible to remove the paint without destroying the bricks. In this case it may be best simply to repaint with a brick color.

However, if you are determined to remove the paint, you may have to try several techniques to find the most effective and least destructive method. If the brick is smooth and has many coats of paint, it may be possible to remove most of the paint with an electric heat gun, which looks like a hand-held hair dryer. This heating softens the paint and causes huge blisters, which can then be scraped off with a putty knife.

You will still need to use a chemical paint remover for the remaining specks of paint; test several brands to find the most effective. Some paint removers are very thin and, thus, are unsuitable for vertical surfaces. Some water-washable paint removers leave a gummy residue, which, like rubber cement, is as difficult to remove as the paint itself. Be prepared for a long, tedious job. You will need soft or natural-bristle brushes, steel wool and plenty of paper towels or rags. Do not sandblast or use a wire brush; both methods will damage the brick, and the roughened surface will cause the brick to collect more soot.

While making some repairs on our old house recently, we found some old nails. We have heard that a house can be dated from the nails. How is this done?

Houses cannot be dated accurately using nails alone. However, some building information can be gained from an examination of nails, and changes or additions to the building often can be identified. Before a house can be dated by its nails, a representative sampling of nails from all parts of the building is necessary.

There are three basic types of nails: hand wrought, cut and wire. Hand-wrought nails were made from rectangular strips of iron. They have rough, flat sides, uneven heads, a taper on all four sides and marks from hammer blows. They were widely used in this country from the time of the earliest European settlements to the early 1800s. Because hand-wrought nails were considered superior for certain types of tasks, they continued in more limited use for several decades following the introduction of cut nails, which were cheaper. Thus, many 1800s buildings have both wrought and cut nails in their original construction. Wrought nails are occasionally made today by museum blacksmiths.

Cut nails can have either hammered heads or stamped heads. These nails also are rectangular but are formed by a cutting machine that makes tapered slices from a piece of iron plate, the taper forming both the shank and the point of the nail. These nails generally date from between 1790 and 1830. As nail-making machinery improved, the heads were flattened with a stamp rather than with a hammer. Nails with stamped heads appeared after 1825, and most can hardly be distinguished from modern cut nails, which have slightly rounded heads. (Cut nails are still made today—notably by the Tremont Nail Company of Wareham, Mass.— and are used because of their great holding power.) Improvements in cut nails usually were made first in the smaller nail sizes, and, of course, some nail manufacturers were more advanced than others.

Wire nails are cut from lengths of spooled steel wire rather than from plates. Introduced in the 1850s and perfected by the 1870s, wire nails are cheaper to produce, easier to handle and made in a variety of forms for special uses. The early wire nails had eccentric bulbous heads. The transition from cut to wire nails was more gradual than from wrought to cut, and it was only in the late 1890s that wire nails became dominant. Again, the early improvements were in the smaller nail sizes first.

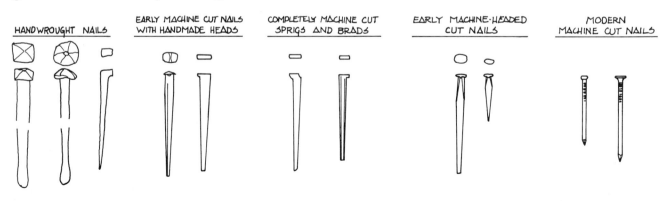

HANDWROUGHT NAILS   EARLY MACHINE CUT NAILS WITH HANDMADE HEADS   COMPLETELY MACHINE CUT SPRIGS AND BRADS   EARLY MACHINE-HEADED CUT NAILS   MODERN MACHINE CUT NAILS

My old house has some interesting brown, marblelike door knobs that have swirls and patterns. Can you tell me what kind of knobs these are? Also, is it possible to replace missing or broken door knobs with similar ones?

From your description it sounds as though your door knobs are "Bennington" door knobs, named after the mottled brown knobs produced at the Bennington (Vt.) pottery factory between 1847 and 1867. These are also called "mineral" knobs. The knobs have clay bodies that have been fired with a glaze to give them the brown marble look you described. These knobs can range from plain brown to greenish brown, depending on the glaze. Some of the striated or marbled ones are the result of deliberate mixing of different clays pressed into the mold. These types are patterned clear through and generally coated with a clear glaze composed mainly of feldspar and flint.

Replacements for your "Bennington" or mineral door knobs can often be found in antiques shops or stores that specialize in architectural antiques. It is also possible to repair broken knobs with epoxy.

I am in the process of restoring my 1916 bungalow and am now ready to tackle the redecoration of the dining room. One of the most interesting features of the room is a horizontal, natural wood molding that extends about 22 inches below the half-timbered ceiling and encircles the room. Vertical strips of wood spaced every 14 inches extend from this horizontal molding to the floor molding and create the effect of wall panels. What kind of decor would be appropriate for a room like this?

Your dining room sounds like a good example of a Craftsman-style house of the first two decades of this century. It may even be copied from a design by Gustav Stickley, who published many designs for such houses in his magazine, *The Craftsman*, during this period. The Craftsman and Mission styles were the distinctly American interpretations of the Arts and Crafts movement in England, which evolved out of the late 19th-century protest against machine-made products. These styles stressed the beauty and creativity expressed in "simple" and "natural" handcrafted materials.

The friezelike space below the ceiling probably was originally covered with wallpaper featuring scenes from nature, a favored motif of the Craftsman style. The frieze may have depicted highly stylized trees of varying heights and widths (such as umbrella-shaped trees alternating with more vertical trees such as poplar or cypress) or flowers, either abstract or realistic. Many reproductions of historic wallpapers are available today, so you should be able to find something suitable that you like. The vertical wall panels below the frieze could be either covered with wallpaper or painted. The ceiling should probably be painted a plain color, perhaps an off-white or cream, in contrast to the darker wood beams. If you like the period effect of the room, you also might want to consider adding Mission-style furniture.

The floors in my 1800 house are random-width heart pine and are in very good condition. I do not plan to refinish the floors, but how should I protect and maintain them?

A good paste-wax finish may be the best treatment for your softwood floors, particularly if they are not splintered or knotty. Polyurethane varnish, which is popular now, is not recommended, because it is too hard a coating for pine, may not take well, scratches easily and will not yield the rich luster your historic floors deserve.

Using a soft cloth, apply the paste wax to a small area of clean floor. Do not try to wax an entire room at once. Allow about five minutes of drying time before buffing with an electric floor polisher. The polished floor can be maintained easily with regular dusting and periodic buffing to renew the shine and to eliminate scuff marks. Do not wax the floor more than two times a year, as too frequent waxing will hasten wax buildup, which will require stripping the floors and starting all over again.

I was told that the wood paneling in my front entrance hall dates from the early 1800s. When I removed some paint from an inconspicuous area as a matter of curiosity, I discovered that the wood had originally been varnished. I do not want to remove all the paint just to expose the wood because the paint seems to have a history of its own. Which approach is best from a preservation standpoint—removing all the paint or leaving it as is?

Ordinarily, you should leave the sequence of paint layers on historic woodwork unless the paint has cracked or peeled. However, in this case, because you have discovered that the original coating was clear, total paint removal is certainly justified. Clear finishes were historically used on hardwoods such as walnut, oak or cherry. Softwoods such as pine and spruce were usually but not always painted. Also, as a result of the higher price of hardwoods, softwoods were sometimes grained, a decorative treatment that simulates the more expensive hardwoods.

The historic district commission of which I am a member increasingly is called on to review both large- and small-scale proposals to enlarge buildings by adding another story. Although we realize that such additions may be an economic necessity in some instances, we are concerned that such projects will destroy the scale of the district. Are there any guidelines we can follow when reviewing such proposals?

Generally, such additions should be discouraged, but occasionally approval of selected projects—for example, the rehabilitation of a vacant building that is an eyesore and that would not otherwise be fixed up—may be in the best interest of the neighborhood. Adding a story to a historic building must be done with sensitivity. The new addition should respect and harmonize with (but not necessarily duplicate) the style, size and materials of the building and of the streetscape as a whole.

An additional story may be added more inconspicuously to a tall building than to a smaller one because the greater distance from the street to the roof makes the addition less prominent and harder to see. Adding a story to a high rise can often be handled successfully with the careful use of setbacks. It is strongly recommended that a new story be of a compatible contemporary design rather than imitate the architectural style of the original building. Compatible contemporary designs should also be used when making discrete roof additions to smaller buildings.

An example of a successful addition is the construction of a third-floor mansard roof on a small house located on a narrow city street lined with two-story, semidetached 1875 brick row houses. A four-story row house, much larger in size and scale and located on a wider thoroughfare, received a fifth floor carefully designed to harmonize with the 1890s Richardsonian Romanesque style of the building and its two neighbors.

We plan to convert our 1890 brick Classical Revival house into five rental apartments, but in order to make the renovation worthwhile economically, the available square footage must be increased. Our architect has suggested treating the new addition as if it were part of the original building—that is, extending the walls, roof and so forth in order to respect all the historic detailing. This idea seems reasonable to us. What do you think?

On the surface this suggestion sounds good, but in reality the flush wall construction and the identical roofing, windows and other decorative detailing will render your once historic house simply imitative. It would be much better (but probably much more difficult for your architect) to design the new construction so that it is clearly different from the existing structure—for example, the addition might have non-Classical Revival details, a setback between the new work and original building and differing roof levels. In short, you will be more respectful of the historic detailing if the addition is compatible with the materials, size, color and texture of your historic house but does not attempt to duplicate them.

I plan to convert an early 19th-century commercial building located downtown near the waterfront into a restaurant. As part of the renovation, I want to install a greenhouse or glassed-in addition to provide extra floor space and to attract business. Do you have any suggestions?

First, you should check with your local zoning or historic district commission to see whether such an addition is possible and, if so, whether it requires a special permit or approval.

Second, make sure the design for the greenhouse is compatible in style and size and harmonious with the architecturally significant aspects of the historic building. The best approach would be to construct a free-standing greenhouse structure or to attach the greenhouse addition at the rear of the building or on an inconspicuous facade where it will not be highly visible. Where the addition is placed depends on how the building is situated on the street and the space available. If the green-house has to be added onto a major street facade, it must be designed so that it intrudes as little as possible on the historic features of the building.

Ideally, the greenhouse construction or treatment should be done in such a manner as to be reversible and should not cause any permanent damage to the historic building fabric. Likewise, the design for the greenhouse should also be as simple as possible (and generally limited in height to one story), so as not to detract from the historic building, which, after all, should be the main subject of attention.

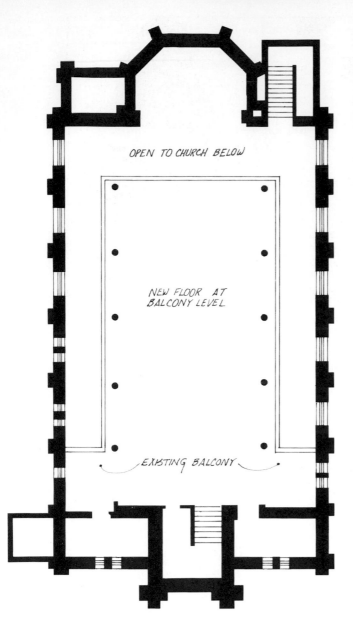

OPEN TO CHURCH BELOW

NEW FLOOR AT BALCONY LEVEL

EXISTING BALCONY

I am thinking about buying an old church that is for sale and developing it for use as commercial office space. The church is an early 20th-century Gothic-style structure and is built of stone. The interior has stained-glass windows and highly ornate capitals decorating clustered piers and columns, and a small balcony (choir stall) stretches across the back of the church. I want to insert another floor level inside the church for maximum rentable office space. Does this sound like a good idea?

Although your desire to save a redundant church is commendable, converting it to office space may not be the most appropriate use or the one most respectful of the church's architectural integrity. Perhaps the neighborhood citizens might support or zoning laws might permit a use other than conversion to offices. Other more sympathetic uses include a small theater or auditorium, concert hall, art gallery, museum, school for performing arts, library, bookstore, orchestra rehearsal hall, social hall, restaurant, shop or display room for antiques, furniture and home furnishings. The only new uses that should be considered seriously are those requiring only simple designs that use the interior space of the church as much as possible in its current form and cause minimal disruption to or destruction of the historic fabric. Such uses would actually enhance or bring out the drama of the space.

However, if office space is the only feasible conversion (because of demand and financial realities), perhaps it could be integrated successfully into the church interior in such a way that would respect the church's integrity. Inserting a second floor in the church would be visually intrusive and would bisect the windows, creating a detrimental visual effect both inside and out. However, you might consider creating a hanging or suspended second floor that, because it would not abut or be totally flush with the side walls and windows, would not be highly visible from the outside. Perhaps the floor could stand on piloti that duplicate or emulate the style of the existing columns and piers. To preserve the sense of openness of the

church interior, it would be even better to consider a two-story center aisle or atrium (i.e., open to the ceiling), perhaps placing along the sides relatively narrow glassed-in "strips" of offices accessible by an open gallery or walkway. This approach would retain the sense of the interior space and permit visibility of the apse.

To reuse a church successfully requires much careful thought and imagination. If you suggest some of these ideas to your architect, he or she might be able to adapt them and come up with a more creative design solution for reusing the church.

I have just purchased a damaged 19th-century row house in Cleveland, Ohio, that has been vacant for several years. Is a renovation using a contemporary design appropriate?

With a severely damaged building, a contemporary approach is often more economical than a conjectural restoration. Usually, however, a few elements of the historic fabric have survived and should be preserved whenever possible. Existing features such as moldings, mantels, newel posts and hardware can usually be restored and serve as a pleasant contrast to a contemporary backdrop. Be sure to preserve elements that may have been covered over, such as skylights over stairwells, which can aid in energy conservation by providing natural light and ventilation. To help preserve the character of the neighborhood and the individuality of the original design, window lintels or hoods that have survived should be retained.

The redevelopment agency in my town is planning to adapt our old Beaux-Arts railroad station as a cultural center. The agency proposes to tear out the floor of the central waiting room, which is flanked on each side by a long, narrow concourse, in order to install a recessed cinema and projection room. I am appalled at the thought of desecrating this grand arched and coffered space in such a manner. Surely there must be a less destructive design approach.

Although rehabilitating the station is commendable, no doubt a theater can be constructed in a less destructive manner. For example, the theater might be better placed in one of the side halls or concourses, which are the right shape and, thus, inherently better suited for projection and audience viewing. If a sloping floor is necessary for better visibility of the screen, installing a temporary slanted platform over the existing floor would be quite simple. The height of these concourses would probably allow for such a platform.

The other option, although not as desirable, would be to construct in the waiting room a free-standing theater space that would be removable and, thus, reversible. Such an adaptation would not destroy either the historic building fabric or the spatial character of the room.

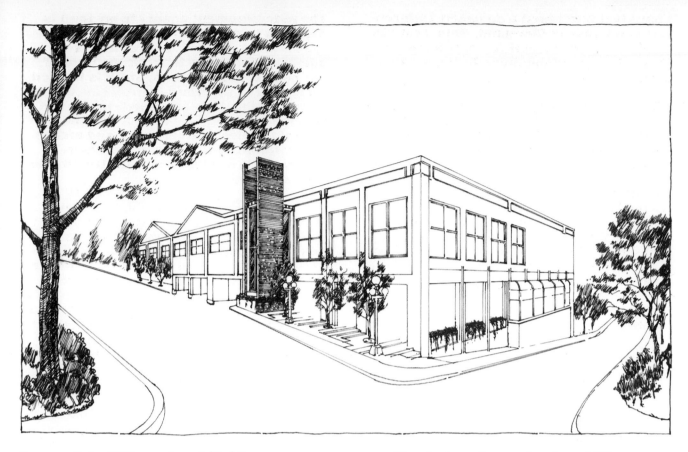

I own a late 19th-century hillside warehouse that I plan to rehabilitate for use as offices. I would like to provide some sort of access to all floors for handicapped persons, but my architect has advised me that the existing structural system will not permit the installation of an interior elevator. It appears that my only alternative is to construct a separate addition on the exterior to house the elevator. How should I approach the design of this addition without disturbing the architectural character of the main building?

In general, you should strive to keep new additions to a minimum, making them compatible in scale, building materials, color and texture with the earlier building and neighborhood. In order to accommodate an elevator addition, choose the least obtrusive location, such as an inconspicuous spot in the rear of the building.

The design of your elevator addition should not detract from the inherent architectural qualities of the main structure. Therefore, a simple, contemporary design solution would be appropriate. The important point is to avoid imitating an earlier style or period for the addition, thus giving the main building a historical appearance it never had. The design should clearly be read as a contemporary feature of the building and not misrepresent itself as a historic element of the property.

The bathroom of our turn-of-the-century farmhouse still has its claw-foot bathtub and marble sink, but it has a modern 1950s toilet. We want to replace the toilet and install one more in keeping with the house and other bathroom fixtures. Where do you suggest we look for a replacement toilet?

Judging from the age of your house and its surviving fixtures, your bathroom originally had a reservoir or high-tank toilet. If you want an authentic toilet, you have two choices. You can attempt to locate a high-tank toilet from a wrecking company or from a dealer who salvages items from old houses that have been demolished; a plumber could then install it. Another alternative, although an expensive one, is to purchase a reproduction high-tank toilet from a large plumbing supply house.

If neither of these options is feasible, you may have to achieve your objective of a period bathroom through skillful decorating. If the existing toilet is not usable and must be replaced, a white fixture should be selected because colored bathroom fixtures were not available when your house was built.

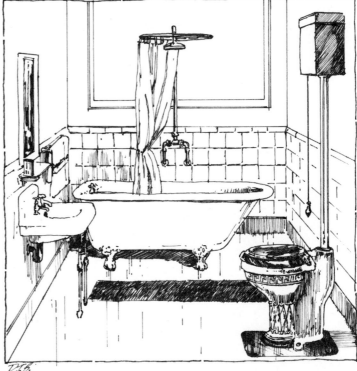

I recently acquired a claw-foot bathtub from a convent that was undergoing modernization. I want to have it installed in my Victorian bathroom, but the finish is in poor condition and the porcelain has a few small chips in it. Can I refinish it with any success?

Yes, you have two options. The first is to resurface the tub yourself using a two-part epoxy system. Clean the porcelain thoroughly by washing it with a trisodium phosphate solution and rinsing with mineral spirits to remove all soap film and other dirt. Fill any chips with an epoxy metal filler. When the filler is completely cured (dry), sand the entire surface with wet-and-dry sandpaper for proper bonding of the second coat and then rinse thoroughly again. Following the manufacturer's directions, apply the first coat of the epoxy and let dry for 24 hours. The second coat should be applied after a light sanding, which is necessary to roughen the surface for proper bonding. Your new finish should last several years before a new application is needed.

You can also have the tub resurfaced professionally. In either case, remember to have the tub resurfaced in white because colored fixtures are a recent innovation and are not appropriate for a historic tub.

The cast-iron radiator in our dining room has a small crack and has begun to leak. We want to keep a radiator in that room because all the other rooms have radiators. Our plumbing contractor, however, has suggested that we replace it with an electric baseboard heating unit because of the difficulty of finding a used radiator in good shape. What do you advise?

Your plumber is right for two reasons about the inadvisability of installing a used radiator. First, because of its age, an old radiator may have or may develop cracks. Repairing cast-iron radiators is difficult; they can crack at the point of repair because of the heating and cooling action as well as from the pressure of the hot water or steam. Second, an old radiator may be so full of scale and rust that it will not heat efficiently.

However, replacing your cracked radiator with an electric baseboard unit is not logical: You would end up with two heating systems, one of which would be heating only one room. A better solution would be to have your plumber install a new cast-iron radiator that will approximate the size and detailing of the damaged one. Cast-iron radiators are still manufactured; you should be able to obtain catalogs from a large plumbing and heating wholesale supply house.

We plan to install fiber-glass batt insulation with a vapor barrier between the attic rafters of our 75-year-old bungalow. (The attic is floored so insulation cannot be placed between the floor joists.) The contractor has suggested replacing the attic's front window with louvers to provide year-round ventilation. We think louvers will look peculiar. Are they necessary?

Attic floors present a problem when weatherizing many older houses. In the case of floored attics, insulation should be placed between the rafters. This method allows the warm, moist air from the occupied portion of the house to flow upward through the house and into the attic. Because of the insulation's vapor barrier (the shiny surface that keeps the insulation dry and that is placed toward the warm air or warm surface), the moisture cannot penetrate the formerly permeable roof sheathing and escape outside. Unless this moisture has access to the outside, it condenses on the cold surfaces of the attic, encouraging fungal growth and eventual decay of the roofing materials. Attics with insulation between the rafters must have adequate year-round ventilation to allow the moisture to escape. As you have discovered, providing for this ventilation can result in the inappropriate placement of ventilators in windows or on the roof.

The overhanging roof characteristic of bungalows provides a good place to hide ventilators. Have the contractor install soffit vents in these areas to let in outside air. A vent should also be placed on the top of the roof to allow moist, warm air to escape. Avoid monitor windows, cupolas and other historically inappropriate designs. Choose a ventilator that is as flush to the roof as possible without letting in rain or snow. Place this ventilator on the top rear slope of the roof so that it will not be visible from the front of the house. If your bungalow has a gable front roof, place the roof vent on the side that is visible from the least traveled side of the street. The ventilation should provide at least 1 square foot of "free area" (amount of open space) for every 300 square feet of attic floor space. This system of ventilation will be more efficient than that suggested by your contractor and will preserve the architectural integrity of your house.

An alternative that would avoid the moisture problems is to install insulation between the attic floor joists. If your attic floor area is small and you do not mind moving any items that are stored in the attic, consider removing the floor, placing the insulation between the joists and then replacing the floor. The warm, moist air will remain in the living space below the attic. Excess moisture will escape through windows and doors during normal use. In addition, the heating system will be more energy efficient, because heated air will be prevented from rising into the unused attic space.

I have recently purchased an 1880s brick house that has two and a half stories. In order to conserve energy, I have been advised to insulate the attic, which is used for storage. What type of insulation should I use?

Assuming that the attic floor joists are open (i.e., there is no permanent floor), you have three choices: (1) blown-in cellulose, (2) poured wool or (3) fiber-glass batts. The latter is often preferred for permanency and performance.

Fiber-glass batts can be purchased in a variety of widths with foil facing, which serves as a vapor barrier. The foil should be placed downward, toward the heated area of the house. Placing the batts between the floor joists will not insulate the attic itself. If you wish to use the attic for something other than inactive storage, a reasonable alternative is to staple the batts to the underside of the roof between the rafters. Regardless of where the batts are placed, a 6-inch layer of fiber-glass insulation should have an R value (thermal resistance) of 19 and will provide a substantial savings on your energy costs.

The crawl space under the back ell of our house, which was built in the 1850s and has a red sandstone foundation, is always wet and smells musty. How can this condition be corrected?

First, try to locate the cause of the dampness. Inspect the gutters and downspouts to see if they are clogged or leaking. If the downspout drains into the city storm sewer, check to see that the sewer pipe is not cracked. If it drains out onto a splash block, be sure the block slopes away from the house. If it drains onto the lawn, make sure the pipe is long enough to draw the water away from the building. It is always a good idea to observe the drainage during a heavy rainstorm. You may simply need to reset the splash block or lengthen the drain pipe. If the back ell has plumbing, check to see that it is not leaking into the crawl space. The crawl space should dry out in several weeks after corrective measures have been taken.

Be sure the crawl space also is well ventilated. Crawl-space vents may have been covered in recent years to prevent heat loss. If so, reopen the vents. You may also wish to speed up evaporation by placing an exhaust fan by one of the vents. If there are no venting holes in the walls, cut in two or four vents, opposite each other, and install venting grilles. Do not cut more vents than you need—the more holes, the colder the crawl space will be in the winter and the more heat you will lose through it.

Once the crawl space has dried out (and if it is accessible), cover the dirt with a 6-mil polyethylene sheet to keep ground moisture out, thereby reducing dampness. If you insulate the floor over the crawl space, be sure to install a vapor barrier on the warm (upper) side of the insulation (i.e., if the insulation is a batt type with a foil face, install it with foil side up). This last step may involve extra expense but will enhance energy efficiency.

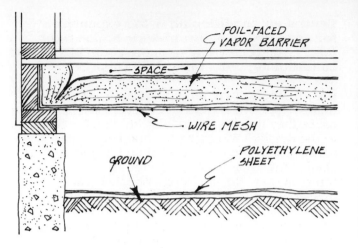

Central air conditioning is too expensive for us to install in our historic house right now. Is there any way to make room air-conditioning units fairly unobtrusive?

Unfortunately, there are no practical ways to make room air conditioners unobtrusive because they must be installed with direct access to the outside. Whether your building is masonry or covered with wood siding, avoid installing the units directly through the wall; room air conditioners have a short life, and this type of installation causes unnecessary damage to the building. If you have windows with double-hung sash, installing the units without damaging historic fabric is a relatively simple task. To minimize the obvious visual impact, install the units in windows on the back or sides of the house, if at all possible. The water that drips from room units should be diverted away from the side of the building; in some cases it may be necessary to add a small hose extension.

Another alternative would be to install a whole-house fan. Although not a substitute for air conditioning, it is a reasonable and inexpensive cooling alternative and can be coupled with a room dehumidifier for increased comfort without the negative visual impact of room air-conditioning units.

I plan to convert a two-story row house into two rental apartments. How should I install a central heating and air-conditioning system so that I do not damage the elaborate crown and baseboard molding and the ceiling medallions on both floors?

Lowering the ceilings to conceal the ductwork would not be appropriate because you want to retain ornamental elements. Considering that different tenants will be on each floor, you could install two separate systems, one in the basement and one in the attic. Ducting in the basement would feed up to the first-floor registers; ducting in the attic would service the second floor through inconspicuous ceiling registers. The disturbance to the ornamentation would be minimal because little chasing through walls would be required. In any case, you should ask an architect or an engineer for assistance.

To conserve energy, my wife and I want to install a solar collector to preheat hot water for our house, which is located in a historic district. Should the collector be placed on the roof or on the ground?

Selection of a site for a solar collector on a historic property depends on two criteria: (1) the visual impact of the equipment on the historic character of the house and the district and (2) the best location for the proper exposure to the sun. Solar collectors, even for preheating hot water, are relatively large and, because of their reflective surface, are an intrusive element, even for houses not in a historic district. For this reason, owners of historic houses prefer to place collectors in inconspicuous areas such as on rear slopes of roofs, behind parapets, on rear facades or in areas of the yard partially hidden by fences, berms or shrubbery.

A second concern in selecting a site for a solar collector is proper installation. Roof-mounted collectors should be securely anchored to the rafters to prevent damage by wind. In addition, the roofing system must have the structural capacity to carry the additional load of the collector. Also, leaking can occur unless those parts of the system that penetrate the building envelope are properly flashed and caulked.

How can I install central air conditioning in my Queen Anne-style frame house? The second floor presents no problem, because ductwork could be laid though the attic space and dropped down through the closets to the second floor. The first floor is a problem, however, because the cellar, where the ductwork would be installed, does not cover the entire house. Where can I put the necessary ductwork for the first floor without it being obtrusive?

If placing the ductwork inside the house would be damaging to the interiors, it could be run through the crawl space between the ground and the first floor. If there is no crawl space, earth could be removed to allow for the ducts. Make sure the ductwork is well insulated before it is placed below the floor.

You have several options that you should investigate. Depending on your floor plan and the amount of architectural detail on your interior walls, you may be able to place the ductwork for a forced air system in the rooms along the interior walls. This solution may not be as visible as might be expected. Ductwork has become much narrower and, thus, less noticeable in the last few years with the development of high-velocity heating, ventilating and air-conditioning systems. Flexible ductwork is also available and may be useful if you have curved walls. When boxed with wallboard and painted the color of each room, it may be surprisingly unobtrusive. Of course, this solution is inappropriate for rooms with historic wallpaper and paneling or rooms in which moldings are an important architectural element. However, it is the least expensive solution and may be appropriate for your house.

If you decide against installing ductwork below the floor, consider installing a chilled water system that uses pipes rather than ductwork. The advantage of this system over forced air is that pipes are much narrower and, hence, less noticeable than ducts. If your house al-

ready has a hot-water heating system, as many older houses do, it can be modified to accept a cooling system. In this case, your radiators would be replaced with baseboard convertors. This type of system has additional benefits: Temperature is more efficiently regulated and the air is less dry than with forced air systems. Unfortunately, this system is also expensive, and you may encounter difficulties finding a heating and cooling contractor willing to adapt an older system.

ATTIC

CRAWL SPACE

BASEMENT

Everything I have read lately about energy conservation in the home states that fireplaces consume more heat than they produce. I have three fireplaces in my old house. Should I stop using them?

The thermal performance and efficiency of fireplaces can be improved in a number of ways. The flow of warm air into the fireplace can be reduced by closing doors into the room where the fire is, thus eliminating the draw of heated air from other rooms. Heat loss is especially serious after the fire has died down and before the damper can be closed. After the fire is out and you are no longer using the room, lay a piece of sheet metal or other noncombustible material against the fireplace opening to prevent the air from being sucked up the chimney. When the fireplace is not in use, inserting a piece of foam rubber above the firebox will cut down on drafts and insulate the opening. (Be sure to remove the foam rubber before you light the fire.)

If your fireplaces do not have dampers, as is the case with very old houses, have them installed. If ready-made dampers do not fit, a blacksmith can probably make some to fit. If possible, install them near the top of the chimney rather than above the firebox. This way, the chimney will remain warm longer after a fire is extinguished and will thus help keep the house warm.

Tempered glass fireplace screens installed on the fireplace opening are a popular method for conserving energy. The screen prevents warm room air from being sucked into the burning fire and up the chimney. These devices have some disadvantages, however. They are fairly expensive and are stylistically incompatible with historic mantels. Moreover, installation can damage fragile fireplace facings such as ceramic tile or marble.

In short, you can continue to enjoy your fireplaces, and, using the methods suggested here, you can reduce heat lost from your fireplaces.

I recently purchased a 1903 townhouse that has been stripped of all its light fixtures. Gas pipes and wires protrude from the center of some attractive ceiling medallions. Do these medallions always indicate the location of light fixtures?

Not always. A plaster medallion indicates the designer's desire to add a decorative feature wherever it was believed to be needed. If a light fixture was also required, the medallion often served as a logical base or receptacle. In many instances, light fixtures have been removed from ceiling medallions, as evidenced by a hole in the center of the medallion. A medallion not originally equipped with electrical service should not be adapted as such because the delicate plaster work could be damaged during the process. In the case of your ceiling medallions—where gas pipes and wires are clearly present, indicating a previous existence of light fixtures—the installation of new electric fixtures is certainly acceptable. The gas pipes can easily be cut off during the electrification procedure.

We are installing new wall light switches in our 1920s bungalow and have discovered frayed and crumbling wiring. Our electrician says that the entire house should be rewired because of the danger of fire. Is there an alternative to such an expensive solution?

In old houses most wiring is made up of BX cable, a metal spiral casing around two or more rubber-insulated wires. Air infiltrating the switch box has caused the rubber insulation to deteriorate, increasing the possibility of short circuits or sparks. In all likelihood, the rest of the insulation within the metal casing is sound.

Before making a decision to rewire your house—which probably is the best solution—the following procedures can be carried out by your electrician. Remove the switch box to see how much slack the wire has. If there is about one foot or more, cut off the deteriorated section, expose new wire, reconnect the switch box and install the new switch. If there is not enough slack, cut away some plaster and then the deteriorated section, add a junction box and new BX cable splice and reconnect the switch box. This solution would be less costly and would extend the life of your wiring by a number of years.

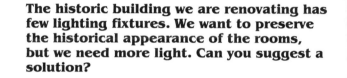

The historic building we are renovating has few lighting fixtures. We want to preserve the historical appearance of the rooms, but we need more light. Can you suggest a solution?

If the original light fixtures are operable, consider using them. Avoid removing historic or distinctive architectural features. If replacements or additional units are required, make every effort to obtain compatible reproductions or replacements. An evaluation of the entire electrical system may be necessary to determine the condition of wiring and the upgrading necessary.

Incorporating contemporary fixtures into the historic fabric without attracting attention to them is sometimes possible. Because the physical conditions of each preservation project vary, it is difficult to be specific about the possibilities. Positioning fixtures on the ceilings or walls may be impossible. If so, you may then want to consider using task lighting, such as movable desk or floor lamps, which can also provide ambient (indirect) lighting.

How can an electrified chandelier be securely mounted in my old house?

Chandeliers are usually mounted in one of two ways: (1) They can be suspended from a large hook screwed directly into a ceiling joist through the ceiling plaster, or (2) they can be screwed onto a threaded receptacle projecting through the ceiling. The disadvantage of both methods is that the fixture tends to become unscrewed and, hence, unstable. One common cause of instability is routine cleaning that can slowly, over several years, twist the fixture until it has no support left. Most chandeliers attached in the second manner have an additional security device, such as a cotter pin or set screw, that should prevent the fixture from unscrewing, but sometimes these are broken off or removed.

 The safest approach would be to inspect carefully the ceiling mount to determine whether the fixture is securely mounted. If it is not, you may need to call in a handyman or perhaps an electrician to repair or strengthen the mounting device.

We have a small house museum and would like to provide access for the handicapped. The front entrance is the most logical place to put a ramp because it has only two steps. However, the three designs contractors have submitted call for construction of ramps that will do considerable damage to the wrought-iron porch rail and hand rail. Can you suggest an alternative solution?

You might be able to use a portable ramp, which can provide access while preserving the building fabric. To be portable and easily usable, such ramps are limited to a size that can overcome only a few steps (approximately 15 vertical inches). They must be constructed to accommodate or fit over the steps beneath. Portability also limits the length of the sections; thus, two- or three-piece ramp decks are the most common. In many cases the slope of portable ramps is so steep that handicapped persons cannot gain entrance unaided.

The use of portable ramps seldom results in damage to historic materials. However, because the design is based on achieving portability and not visual sensitivity, ramps can detract from a building's historic appearance. When not in use, the ramp can be disassembled and stored, for example, under an adjacent porch.

My wife must now use a wheelchair, so we plan to have an entrance ramp constructed for her. We can use the garden entrance, as the door sill is only three feet above the garden walk. What length of ramp is recommended for this entrance height?

A wheelchair ramp should rise no more than 1 inch per foot, an 8 percent grade. Thus your ramp length should be at least 36 feet long. Moreover, a resting platform is required for a ramp longer than 30 feet. If you have enough space in your side yard, you may want to create a U-shaped ramp, or you might want to consider using a compact, electrically powered wheelchair lift. The lift, which is about 3 by 6 feet and costs about $1,000 to install, can be nestled beside the stoop to the entrance and attractively landscaped to reduce its impact on the garden.

In researching my 1894 house in Charleston, S.C., I came across several articles on the disastrous Charleston earthquake of 1889. My house is extremely well built—it is a simple rectangular form, two and a half stories high, and has heavy masonry walls, large wooden floor timbers and a substantial slate roof. I know that houses can be seismically reinforced, but I also have heard that the process is expensive and can cause quite a bit of damage to the historic fabric of the house. Should I consider this modification for safety?

The general philosophy of seismic construction is to keep the configuration of the building simple and to tie together all the parts. Your building meets the first requirement—sound construction—but this fact does not offset the need to tie everything together should you decide to reinforce the house seismically. In fact, if there were a major earthquake in Charleston, chances are that the heavy masonry walls would fall outward, causing the large timbers and enormously heavy slate roof to come crashing down.

Seismic reinforcement acts to tie together the vertical and horizontal components of a building (columns, beams and floor joists). Its basic principle is the insertion of a rigid frame of beams, angles and columns to connect the

floor joists and roof to the wall. The masonry walls are tied to the diagonal bracing in the frame to ensure that the walls do not peel away from the building.

For each building a qualified engineer could make several complex designs for seismic reinforcing based on the characteristics of the seismic zone in which the building is located. The important thing to remember about seismic reinforcement is that the inserted rigid frame is intended as a life-safety feature and is not intended to ensure that the building survives an earthquake undamaged.

My architectural firm has just been commissioned to design the renovation of a large turn-of-the-century office building. The building itself, although quite run-down now, was once elegant and still has a number of Beaux-Arts decorative features. The most notable are elaborate cast- and wrought-iron stairways and an open-cage elevator. Is it possible to save these features and still meet the local building code regulations?

Yes, a compromise should be possible. Fire and safety code requirements, especially those pertaining to the rehabilitation of older or historic buildings, vary considerably from one part of the country to another. Most existing building codes were developed with new construction in mind. Seldom do building codes take into consideration their impact, often adverse, on the design and materials of historic buildings.

However, in some communities special, less rigid building codes are gradually being adopted and applied to historic buildings. For instance, some owners of historic buildings faced with similar problems have been able successfully to meet code requirements by enclosing open staircases or elevators with clear, fire-rated glass and glass fire doors or, in some cases, merely by installing a sprinkler system. If space allows, you might be able to install a supplementary modern elevator, retaining the original merely as a decorative feature.

Although these solutions may not be totally satisfactory and may still, to some extent, detract from the stylistic character of these features, they are preferable to the alternative—demolition or removal. Because of the vagaries of building codes, you should discuss the matter with the local building inspectors and code officials. In this way perhaps you will be able to arrive at a treatment of the staircases and elevator that is attractive, safe and mutually acceptable. It might also be helpful to consult other architects and preservation groups in your area who have experienced similar problems in rehabilitating historic buildings.

I am converting a three-story, 1892 Queen Anne-style house to six apartments. The original main stairway will be used for primary access to the four upstairs units, but the city requires that I provide a second means of egress from each unit. Where should I place the fire stairs so that they have minimal impact on the historic character of the building?

It goes without saying that the fire egress stairs should not be built on major facades of a historic building. As long as no significant features or spaces (e.g., door or window trim, mantels, parquet floors and so forth) are disturbed, one solution would be to build a fire-rated stairway inside the house. Another would

be to build an exterior structure, either open or enclosed, on a rear or insignificant side elevation. The type of structure, its design and the materials used in its construction will be dictated by your budget and by the requirements imposed by the local code officials. Whatever the design, however, the size of the structure should not overwhelm your building. If possible, it should be built out of sight of public rights-of-way; it should be constructed of materials compatible with the historic building; and it should be painted a color that will help it blend in with the building.

I think that the loose insulation in the attic of the old house I recently bought might be asbestos. How can I tell whether it is asbestos? If it is, what is the best way to remove it?

Before the U.S. Environmental Protection Agency banned asbestos for certain residential uses, it was used in many houses to insulate attics and boilers, cover pipes and patch walls. The health hazards posed by inhaling the microscopic particles of asbestos are well documented and include lung cancer, asbestosis and other respiratory diseases.

To find out whether the substance in your house is asbestos, contact a housing inspector, heating contractor, local environmental health official or local testing firm. If you do have loose asbestos insulation, have a contractor vacuum it out (after sealing the attic to prevent particles from escaping into the house during the vacuuming). Your local health department may maintain a file of firms qualified to remove asbestos.

Under no circumstances should anyone attempt to remove asbestos without adequate protective clothing and proper equipment, including plastic coveralls and boots, goggles, respirators capable of filtering the particles and special vacuum cleaners capable of capturing and holding airborne asbestos dust. (To avoid lawsuits, house owners should insist that workers be properly outfitted.)

Asbestos used both inside and outside the house can also be hazardous. A professional should check pipe wrappings, for example, to ensure that they are not loose, torn or cracked. Asbestos siding should be kept painted to trap particles and should not be sanded or scraped.

For further information, contact the Consumer Product Safety Commission, Washington, D.C. 20207.

The warehouse I recently bought has been abandoned for many years and is heavily contaminated with pigeon excrement. Is this excrement a health threat? If so, what should I do about it?

Accumulations of pigeon excrement in old buildings can act as a medium for the development of the pathogenic fungi that cause cryptococcosis or histoplasmosis, both potentially fatal diseases of the lungs and central nervous system. These diseases can be latent—in other words, symptoms may not develop until several years after contact. If you have already entered a building containing significant accumulations of bird excrement, have your physician test you for these two diseases. They can be treated successfully if diagnosed at an early stage.

The organisms that cause the diseases are airborne, so when entering buildings containing accumulations of bird excrement, always wear coveralls or other protective clothing and footwear that are disposable or that can be decontaminated separately. Use a breathing mask capable of screening out particles 1 micron or greater; the mask should be the last item removed after leaving a building.

Although the fungi that cause these diseases do not always develop in buildings containing accumulations of excrement, professional health officials should conduct necessary tests. For advice about having samples tested, you should contact your local health department. If it is unable to perform the tests, contact the Center for Disease Control, U.S. Public Health Service, Atlanta, Ga. 30333, for further assistance.

Two years ago I insulated my frame farmhouse with urea-formaldehyde foam. I heard on the news the other night that this type of insulation can present health hazards and that future installations have been banned. How can I go about getting it out?

As you probably learned, the problems posed by urea-formaldehyde foam for both the inhabitants of a house and the house itself are enormous. After investigating numerous cases of chronic and acute illness reported by inhabitants of houses insulated with urea-formaldehyde foam, the U.S. Consumer Product Safety Commission has determined that urea-formaldehyde foam can present serious health hazards to occupants. Consequently, several states have banned the use of urea-formaldehyde foam insulation; others are considering such a step.

Urea-formaldehyde foam is no less harmful to the buildings themselves. The foam, which has the consistency of shaving cream, is injected wet into the frame structure. As it dries, or cures, as many as five quarts of water for each stud cavity (of approximately 2 by 8 feet) are released and must be absorbed by adjacent materials. Moisture is one of the worst problems for an old building, and the excess moisture released by the foam can result in rotten wood members, fungus growths within walls, damp plaster and blistering and peeling paint. In some cases it can rust metal elements within the wall (such as nails, metal lath, electrical fittings and anchoring devices). In addition, standing water can accumulate on the structural wood sills, thus creating the potential for severe damage.

Unfortunately, there is only one way to remove urea-formaldehyde foam—open up the walls of the house and scrape out the dried foam. This process entails removing the siding from the exterior or removing the plaster from the interior of the house. Before undertaking the expensive and destructive process of removing the foam, you should try to find out whether formaldehyde gas is being given off into your house and whether the water injected with the foam is damaging the building material. A building contractor can determine the extent of moisture damage. Local health department officials or commercial laboratories should be able to assist you in testing for the presence of gas (look in the Yellow Pages under "laboratories"). The preferred testing method is the chromotropic acid method recommended by the National Institute of Occupational Safety and Health. If you are unable to obtain such assistance in your area, you can try any of several commercially marketed tests.

For further information about possible corrective measures, contact the Consumer Product Safety Commission, Washington, D.C. 20207.

I have heard a lot about the hazards of children accidentally eating chips of lead paint that fall from interior walls or windowsills. Is it not true that the body can absorb lead in other ways?

Yes. The lead in lead paint can be ingested by swallowing the dust caused by scraping or sanding during paint removal. Therefore, when performing these tasks, be sure to wear a toxic-dust respirator, specified by the paint manufacturer, that filters out lead. You can also inhale lead if lead is vaporized; the intense heat of a blowtorch, for example, causes lead paint to vaporize. Thus, the blowtorch is not recommended as a paint-removal device because it can burn historic building materials, such as wood, and is a potential health and safety hazard.

The Secretary of the Interior's Standards for Rehabilitation

The following Standards for Rehabilitation, developed by Technical Preservation Services, U.S. Department of the Interior, apply to the rehabilitation of all historic and other old buildings. The standards are intended to create a strong framework for responsible preservation practices, to be used in conjunction with the accompanying guidelines for applying the standards. The underlying concern of the standards is the preservation of the significant historic and architectural characteristics of a structure that is being rehabilitated.

In addition to providing guidance to individual property owners as they plan their rehabilitation work, the standards are used by the Secretary of the Interior to determine whether a rehabilitation project qualifies as a ''certified rehabilitation'' for federal tax benefits under the Economic Recovery Tax Act of 1981. They are also used to assist state and local governments and individuals in planning and carrying out rehabilitation work on historic buildings.

The Standards for Rehabilitation make up one section in the comprehensive Secretary of the Interior's Standards for Historic Preservation Projects and appear in Title 36 of the Code of Federal Regulations, Part 68.

1.   Every reasonable effort shall be made to provide a compatible use for a property which requires minimal alteration of the building, structure or site and its environment, or to use a property for its originally intended purpose.

2.   The distinguishing original qualities or character of a building, structure or site and its environment shall not be destroyed. The removal or alteration of any historic material or distinctive architectural features should be avoided when possible.

3.   All buildings, structures and sites shall be recognized as products of their own time. Alterations that have no historical basis and which seek to create an earlier appearance shall be discouraged.

4.   Changes which may have taken place in the course of time are evidence of the history and development of a building, structure or site and its environment. These changes may have acquired significance in their own right, and this significance shall be recognized and respected.

5.   Distinctive stylistic features or examples of skilled craftsmanship which characterize a building, structure or site shall be treated with sensitivity.

6.   Deteriorated architectural features shall be repaired rather than replaced, wherever possible. In the event replacement is necessary, the new material should match the material being replaced in composition, design, color, texture and other visual qualities. Repair or replacement of missing architectural features should be based on accurate duplications of features, substantiated by historic, physical or pictorial evidence rather than on conjectural designs or the availability of different architectural elements from other buildings or structures.

7.   The surface cleaning of structures shall be undertaken with the gentlest means possible. Sandblasting and other cleaning methods that will damage the historic building materials shall not be undertaken.

8.   Every reasonable effort shall be made to protect and preserve archeological resources affected by or adjacent to any project.

9.   Contemporary design for alterations and additions to existing properties shall not be discouraged when such alterations and additions do not destroy significant historical, architectural or cultural material, and such design is compatible with the size, scale, color, material and character of the property, neighborhood or environment.

10.   Wherever possible, new additions or alterations to structures shall be done in such a manner that if such additions or alterations were to be removed in the future, the essential form and integrity of the structure would be unimpaired.

Guidelines for Rehabilitating Historic Buildings

These guidelines for applying the Secretary of the Interior's Standards for Rehabilitation are designed to help individual property owners formulate plans for the rehabilitation, preservation and continued use of historic buildings consistent with the intent of the standards. The guidelines pertain to buildings of all occupancy and construction types, sizes and materials. They apply to permanent and temporary construction on the exterior and interior of historic buildings as well as new attached or adjacent construction.

Techniques, treatments and methods consistent with the Secretary's Standards for Rehabilitation are listed in the "recommended" column on the left. Not all recommendations listed under a treatment will apply to each project proposal. Rehabilitation approaches, materials and methods that may adversely affect a building's architectural and historic qualities are listed in the "not recommended" column on the right. Every effort will be made to update and expand the guidelines as additional techniques and treatments become known.

Specific information on rehabilitation and preservation technology may be obtained by writing to Technical Preservation Services, National Park Service, U.S. Department of the Interior, Washington, D.C. 20240, or the appropriate state historic preservation office; see also Reading About Rehabilitation (p. 173). Advice should also be sought from qualified professionals, including architects, architectural historians and archeologists skilled in the preservation, restoration and rehabilitation of old buildings.

THE ENVIRONMENT

Recommended	*Not Recommended*
Retaining distinctive features such as the size, scale, mass, color and materials of buildings, including roofs, porches and stairways, that give a neighborhood its distinguishing character.	Introducing new construction into neighborhoods that is incompatible with the character of the district because of size, scale, color and materials.
Retaining landscape features such as parks, gardens, street lights, signs, benches, walkways, streets, alleys and building setbacks that have traditionally linked buildings to their environment.	Destroying the relationship of buildings and their environment by widening existing streets, changing paving material or introducing inappropriately located new streets and parking lots that are incompatible with the character of the neighborhood.
Using new plant materials, fencing, walkways, street lights, signs and benches that are compatible with the character of the neighborhood in size, scale, material and color.	Introducing signs, street lighting, benches, new plant materials, fencing, walkways and paving materials that are out of scale or are inappropriate to the neighborhood.

BUILDING SITE

Recommended

Identifying plants, trees, fencing, walkways, outbuildings and other elements that might be an important part of the property's history and development.

Retaining plants, trees, fencing, walkways, street lights, signs and benches that reflect the property's history and development.

Basing decisions for new site work on actual knowledge of the past appearance of the property found in photographs, drawings, newspapers and tax records. If changes are made they should be carefully evaluated in light of the past appearance of the site.

Providing proper site and roof drainage to ensure that water does not splash against building or foundation walls or drain toward the building.

Not Recommended

Making changes to the appearance of the site by removing old plants, trees, fencing, walkways, outbuildings and other elements before evaluating their importance in the property's history and development.

Leaving plant materials and trees in close proximity to the building that may be causing deterioration of the historic fabric.

Archeological Features

Recommended

Leaving known archeological resources intact.

Minimizing disturbance of terrain around the structure, thus reducing the possibility of destroying unknown archeological resources.

Arranging for an archeological survey of all terrain that must be disturbed during the rehabilitation program. The survey should be conducted by a professional archeologist.

Not Recommended

Installing underground utilities, pavements and other modern features that disturb archeological resources.

Introducing heavy machinery or equipment into areas where their presence may disturb archeological resources.

STRUCTURAL SYSTEMS

Recommended

Recognizing the special problems inherent in the structural systems of historic buildings, especially where there are visible signs of cracking, deflection or failure.

Undertaking stabilization and repair of weakened structural members and systems.

Replacing historically important structural members only when necessary. Supplementing existing structural systems when damaged or inadequate.

Not Recommended

Disturbing existing foundations with new excavations that undermine the structural stability of the building.

Leaving untreated known structural problems that will cause continuing deterioration and will shorten the life of the structure.

MASONRY: ADOBE, BRICK, STONE, TERRA COTTA, CONCRETE, STUCCO AND MORTAR

Recommended

Retaining original masonry and mortar, whenever possible, without the application of any surface treatment.

Repointing only those mortar joints where there is evidence of moisture problems or where sufficient mortar is missing to allow water to stand in the mortar joint.

Duplicating old mortar in composition, color and texture.

Duplicating old mortar in joint size, method of application and joint profile.

Repairing stucco with a stucco mixture that duplicates the original as closely as possible in appearance and texture.

Not Recommended

Applying waterproof or water-repellent coatings or surface consolidation treatments unless required to solve a specific technical problem that has been studied and identified. Coatings are frequently unnecessary, expensive and can accelerate deterioration of the masonry.

Repointing mortar joints that do not need repointing. Using electric saws and hammers to remove mortar can seriously damage the adjacent brick.

Repointing with mortar of high portland cement content can often create a bond that is stronger than the building material. This can cause deterioration as a result of the differing coefficient of expansion and the differing porosity of the material and the mortar.

Repointing with mortar joints of a differing size or joint profile, texture or color.

Recommended

Cleaning masonry only when necessary to halt deterioration or to remove graffiti and stains and always with the gentlest method possible, such as low pressure water and soft natural-bristle brushes.

Repairing or replacing, where necessary, deteriorated material with new material that duplicates the old as closely as possible.

Replacing missing significant architectural features, such as cornices, brackets, railings and shutters.

Retaining the original or early color and texture of masonry surfaces, including early signage wherever possible. Brick or stone surfaces may have been painted or whitewashed for practical and aesthetic reasons.

Not Recommended

Sandblasting, including dry and wet grit and other abrasives, brick or stone surfaces; this method of cleaning erodes the surface of the material and accelerates deterioration. Using chemical cleaning products that would have an adverse chemical reaction with the masonry materials, e.g., acid on limestone or marble.

Applying new material that is inappropriate or was unavailable when the building was constructed, such as artificial brick siding, artificial cast stone or brick veneer.

Removing architectural features such as cornices, brackets, railings, shutters, window architraves and doorway pediments.

Removing paint from masonry surfaces indiscriminately. This may subject the building to damage and change its appearance.

WOOD: CLAPBOARD, WEATHERBOARD, SHINGLES AND OTHER WOODEN SIDING

Recommended

Retaining and preserving significant architectural features, whenever possible.

Repairing or replacing, where necessary, deteriorated components with material that duplicates the old as closely as possible in size, shape and texture.

Not Recommended

Removing architectural features such as siding, cornices, brackets, window architraves and doorway pediments. These are, in most cases, an essential part of a building's character and appearance that illustrate the continuity of growth and change.

Resurfacing frame buildings with new material that is inappropriate or was unavailable when the building was constructed, such as artificial stone, brick veneer, asbestos or asphalt shingles, and plastic or aluminum siding. Such material can also contribute to the deterioration of the structure from moisture and insects.

ARCHITECTURAL METALS: CAST IRON, STEEL, PRESSED TIN, ALUMINUM AND ZINC

Recommended

Retaining original material, whenever possible.

Cleaning when necessary with the appropriate method. Metals should be cleaned by methods that do not abrade the surface.

Not Recommended

Removing architectural features that are an essential part of a building's character and appearance, illustrating the continuity of growth and change.

Exposing metals that were intended to be protected from the environment. Do not use cleaning methods that alter the color, texture and tone of the metal.

ROOFS AND ROOFING

Recommended

Preserving the original roof shape.

Retaining the original roofing material, whenever possible.

Providing adequate roof drainage and ensuring that the roofing materials provide a weathertight covering for the structure.

Replacing deteriorated roof coverings with new material that matches the old in composition, size, shape, color and texture.

Preserving or replacing where necessary all architectural features that give the roof its essential character, such as dormer windows, cupolas, cornices, brackets, chimneys, cresting and weather vanes.

Not Recommended

Changing the essential character of the roof by adding inappropriate features such as dormer windows, vents or skylights.

Applying new roofing material that is inappropriate to the style and period of the building and neighborhood.

Replacing deteriorated roof coverings with new materials that differ to such an extent from the old in composition, size, shape, color and texture that the appearance of the building is altered.

Stripping the roof of architectural features important to its character.

WINDOWS AND DOORS

Recommended

Retaining and repairing window and door openings, frames, sash, glass, doors, lintels, sills, pediments, architraves, hardware, awnings and shutters where they contribute to the architectural and historic character of the building.

Improving the thermal performance of existing windows and doors through adding or replacing weatherstripping and adding storm windows and doors that are compatible with the character of the building and that do not damage window or door frames.

Replacing missing or irreparable windows on significant facades with new windows that match the original in material, size, general muntin and mullion proportion and configuration, and reflective qualities of the glass.

Not Recommended

Introducing or changing the location or size of windows, doors and other openings that alter the architectural and historic character of the building.

Replacing window and door features on significant facades with historically and architecturally incompatible materials such as anodized aluminum and mirrored or tinted glass.

Removing window and door features that can be repaired where such features contribute to the historic and architectural character of the building.

Changing the size or arrangement of window panes, muntins and rails where they contribute to the architectural and historic character of the building.

Installing on significant facades shutters, screens, blinds, security grilles and awnings that are historically inappropriate and that detract from the character of the building.

Installing new exterior storm windows and doors that are inappropriate in size or color, are inoperable or require removal of original windows and doors.

Installing interior storm windows that allow moisture to accumulate and damage the window.

Replacing sash that contribute to the character of a building with those that are incompatible in size, configuration and reflective qualities or that alter the setback relationship between window and wall.

Installing heating and air-conditioning units in the window frames when the sash and frames may be damaged. Window installations should be considered only when all other viable heating and cooling systems would result in significant damage to historic materials.

STOREFRONTS

Recommended

Retaining and repairing existing storefronts including windows, sash, doors, transoms, signage and decorative features where such features contribute to the architectural and historic character of the building.

Where original or early storefronts no longer exist or are too deteriorated to save, retaining the commercial character of the building through (1) contemporary design that is compatible with the scale, design, materials, color and texture of the historic buildings, or (2) an accurate restoration of the storefront based on historical research and physical evidence.

Not Recommended

Introducing a storefront or new design element on the ground floor, such as an arcade that alters the architectural and historic character of the building and its relationship with the street or its setting or that causes destruction of significant historic fabric.

Using materials that detract from the historic or architectural character of the building, such as mirrored glass.

Altering the entrance through a significant storefront.

ENTRANCES, PORCHES AND STEPS

Recommended

Retaining porches and steps that are appropriate to the building and its development. Porches or additions reflecting later architectural styles are often important to the building's historical integrity and, wherever possible, should be retained.

Repairing or replacing, where necessary, deteriorated architectural features of wood, iron, cast iron, terra cotta, tile and brick.

Not Recommended

Removing or altering porches and steps that are appropriate to the building's development and style.

Stripping porches and steps of original material and architectural features, such as hand rails, balusters, columns, brackets and roof decoration of wood, iron, cast iron, terra cotta, tile and brick.

Enclosing porches and steps in a manner that destroys their intended appearance.

EXTERIOR FINISHES

Recommended

Discovering the historic paint colors and finishes of the structure and repainting with those colors to illustrate the distinctive character of the property.

Not Recommended

Removing paint and finishes down to the bare surface; strong paint strippers, whether chemical or mechanical, can permanently damage the surface. Also, stripping obliterates evidence of the historical paint finishes.

Repainting with colors that cannot be documented through research and investigation to be appropriate to the building and neighborhood.

INTERIOR FEATURES

Recommended

Retaining, whenever possible, original material, architectural features and hardware, such as stairs, elevators, hand rails, balusters, ornamental columns, cornices, baseboards, doors, doorways, windows, mantelpieces, paneling, lighting fixtures and parquet or mosaic flooring.

Repairing or replacing, where necessary, deteriorated material with new material that duplicates the old as closely as possible.

Retaining original plaster, whenever possible.

Discovering and retaining original paint colors, wallpapers and other decorative motifs or, where necessary, replacing them with colors, wallpapers or decorative motifs based on the original.

Not Recommended

Removing original material, architectural features and hardware, except where essential for safety or efficiency.

Replacing interior doors and transoms without investigating alternative fire protection measures or possible code variances.

Installing new decorative material and paneling that destroys significant architectural features or was unavailable when the building was constructed, such as vinyl plastic or imitation wood wall and floor coverings, except in utility areas such as bathrooms and kitchens.

Removing plaster to expose brick to give the wall an appearance it never had.

Changing the texture and patina of exposed wooden architectural features (including structural members) and masonry surfaces through sandblasting or use of other abrasive techniques to remove paint, discoloration and plaster, except in certain industrial or warehouse buildings where the interior masonry or plaster surfaces do not have significant design, detailing, tooling or finish, and where wooden architectural features are not finished, molded, beaded or worked by hand.

INTERIOR FEATURES—*continued*

Recommended

Where required by code, enclosing an important interior stairway in such a way as to retain its character. In many cases glazed fire-rated walls may be used.

Retaining the basic plan of a building, the relationship and size of rooms, corridors and other spaces.

Not Recommended

Enclosing important stairways with ordinary fire-rated construction that destroys the architectural character of the stair and the space.

Altering the basic plan of a building by demolishing principal walls, partitions and stairways.

NEW CONSTRUCTION

Recommended

Keeping new additions and adjacent new construction to a minimum, making them compatible in scale, building materials and texture.

Designing new work to be compatible in materials, size, color and texture with the earlier building and the neighborhood.

Using contemporary designs compatible with the character and mood of the building or the neighborhood.

Not Recommended

Designing new work that is incompatible with the earlier building and the neighborhood in materials, size, scale and texture.

Imitating an earlier style or period of architecture in new additions, except in rare cases where a contemporary design would detract from the architectural unity of an ensemble or group. Especially avoid imitating an earlier style of architecture in new additions that have a completely contemporary function such as a drive-in bank or garage.

Adding new height to the building that changes the scale and character of the building. Additions in height should not be visible when viewing the principal facades.

Adding new floors or removing existing floors that destroy important architectural details, features and spaces of the building.

Protecting architectural details and features that contribute to the character of the building.

Placing television antennae and mechanical equipment, such as air conditioners, in an inconspicuous location.

Placing television antennae and mechanical equipment, such as air conditioners, where they can be seen from the street.

MECHANICAL SYSTEMS: HEATING, AIR CONDITIONING, ELECTRICAL, PLUMBING AND FIRE PROTECTION

Recommended

Installing necessary mechanical systems in areas and spaces that will require the least possible alteration to the structural integrity and physical appearance of the building.

Utilizing early mechanical systems, including plumbing and early lighting fixtures, where possible.

Installing the vertical runs of ducts, pipes and cables in closets, service rooms and wall cavities.

Ensuring adequate ventilation of attics, crawl spaces and cellars to prevent moisture problems.

Installing thermal insulation in attics and in unheated cellars and crawl spaces to conserve energy.

Not Recommended

Causing unnecessary damage to the plan, materials and appearance of the building when installing mechanical systems.

Attaching exterior electrical and telephone cables to the principal elevations of the building.

Installing vertical runs of ducts, pipes and cables in places where they will be a visual intrusion.

Concealing or making invisible mechanical equipment in historic walls or ceilings. Frequently this concealment requires the removal of historic fabric.

Installing dropped acoustical ceilings to hide mechanical equipment. This destroys the proportions and character of the rooms.

Installing foam, fiber-glass or cellulose insulation in wall cavities of either wooden or masonry construction. This has been found to cause moisture problems when there is no adequate moisture barrier.

SAFETY AND CODE REQUIREMENTS

Recommended

Complying with code requirements in such a manner that the essential character of a building is preserved intact.

Working with local code officials to investigate alternative life safety measures that preserve the architectural integrity of the building.

Investigating variances for historic properties allowed under some local codes.

Installing adequate fire prevention equipment in a manner that does minimal damage to the appearance or fabric of a property.

Adding new stairways and elevators that do not alter existing exit facilities or other important architectural features and spaces of the building.

Not Recommended

Adding new stairways and elevators that alter existing exit facilities or important architectural features and spaces of the building.

READING ABOUT REHABILITATION

Getting Started: *General Sources*

Anthony, Aubra H., Jr. "Summary of Preservation Tax Incentives in the Economic Recovery Tax Act of 1981." Information Series, no. 30. Washington, D.C.: Preservation Press, 1981.

Blumenson, John J.G. *Identifying American Architecture: A Pictorial Guide to Styles and Terms, 1600–1945.* l977. 2nd ed. Nashville: American Association for State and Local History, 1981.

Derry, Anne, et al. National Register of Historic Places, U.S. Department of the Interior. *Guidelines for Local Surveys: A Basis for Preservation Planning.* Washington, D.C.: U.S. Government Printing Office, 1977. GPO stock no. 024-016-0089-7.

Fisher, Charles E., William G. MacRostie and Christopher A. Sowick. "Directory of Historic Preservation Easement Organizations." Washington, D.C.: Technical Preservation Services Division, U.S. Department of the Interior, 1981.

Friedland, Edward P. *Antique Houses: Their Construction and Restoration.* Garden City, N.Y.: Doubleday, 1981.

Grow, Lawrence, ed. *The Third Old House Catalogue.* New York: Macmillan, 1982.

Hecker, John C., AIA, and Sylvanus W. Doughty. *Planning for Exterior Work on the First Parish Church, Portland, Maine: Using Photographs as Project Documentation.* Preservation Case Studies. Technical Preservation Services Division, U.S. Department of the Interior. Washington, D.C.: U.S. Government Printing Office, 1979. GPO stock no. 024-016-00210-6.

Hotton, Peter. *So You Want to Fix Up an Old House.* Boston: Little, Brown, 1979.

International Centre for Conservation and International Centre Committee, Advisory Council on Historic Preservation. *Preservation and Conservation: Principles and Practices.* Washington, D.C.: Preservation Press, 1976.

Judd, Henry A. "Before Restoration Begins: Keeping Your Historic House Intact." Technical Leaflet Series, no. 67. Nashville: American Association for State and Local History, 1973.

Kleyle, Frederec E., ed. "Rehabilitation of Historic Buildings: An Annotated Bibliography." Technical Preservation Services Division, U.S. Department of the Interior. Washington, D.C.: U.S. Government Printing Office, 1980. GPO stock no. 024-016-00130-3.

Labine, Clem, and Carolyn Flaherty, eds. *The Old-House Journal Compendium.* Woodstock, N.Y.: Overlook Press, Viking, 1980.

Old-House Journal Editors. *The Old-House Journal 1982 Catalog: A Buyers' Guide.* Brooklyn, N.Y.: Author, with Overlook Press, Viking, 1981.

Phillips, Morgan W. "The Eight Most Common Mistakes in Restoring Houses (and How to Avoid Them)." Technical Leaflet Series, no. 118. Nashville: American Association for State and Local History, 1979.

Poppeliers, John C., S. Allen Chambers and Nancy B. Schwartz. *What Style Is It?* Washington, D.C.: Preservation Press, 1977.

Reader's Digest Association. *Reader's Digest Complete Do-It-Yourself Manual.* New York: Author, 1973.

Rooney, William F., and Hudson Home Magazine Editors. *Practical Guide to Home Restoration.* New York: Van Nostrand Reinhold, 1980.

Saxe, Emma Jane. "How to Qualify Historic Properties Under the New Federal Law Affecting Easements." National Register of Historic Places. *How To* Series. Washington, D.C.: National Park Service, U.S. Department of the Interior, 1981.

Stanforth, Deirdre, and Martha Stamm. *Buying and Renovating a House in the City: A Practical Guide.* New York: Alfred A. Knopf, 1972.

Stephen, George. *Remodeling Old Houses Without Destroying Their Character.* New York: Alfred A. Knopf, 1972.

Technical Preservation Services Division, U.S. Department of the Interior. *The Secretary of the Interior's Standards for Historic Preservation Projects, with Guidelines for Applying the Standards.* Washington, D.C.: U.S. Government Printing Office, 1979. GPO stock no. 024-016-00105-2.

Time-Life Editors, *The Old House.* Home Repair and Improvement Series, no. 19. Alexandria, Va.: Time-Life Books, 1979.

Whiffen, Marcus. *American Architecture Since 1780: A Guide to the Styles.* Cambridge, Mass.: MIT Press, 1969.

Periodicals

Bulletin. Quarterly. Association for Preservation Technology, Box 2487, Station D, Ottawa, Ontario K1P 5W6, Canada.

Fine Homebuilding. Bimonthly. Taunton Press, P.O. Box 355, Newton, Conn. 06470.

Historic Preservation. Bimonthly. National Trust for Historic Preservation, 1785 Massachusetts Avenue, N.W., Washington, D.C. 20036.

Old-House Journal. Monthly. Old-House Journal Corporation, 69A Seventh Avenue, Brooklyn, N.Y. 11217.

Restoration Products News. Quarterly. 199 Berkeley Place, Brooklyn, N.Y. 11217.

Technology and Conservation. Quarterly. One Emerson Place, Boston, Mass. 02114.

Victorian Homes. Quarterly. Renovators Supply, P.O. Box 61, Millers Falls, Mass. 01349.

The Environment

Bremer, Terry, and Russell Cohen, comps. *1981 National Directory of Local Land Conservation Organizations.* Boston: Land Trust Exchange, 1982.

Martin, George A., ed. *Fences, Gates and Bridges: A Practical Manual.* 1887. Reprint. Brattleboro, Vt.: Stephen Greene Press, 1974.

Stipe, Robert E., ed. *New Directions in Rural Preservation.* Division of State Plans and Grants, U.S. Department of the Interior. Preservation Planning Series. Washington, D.C.: U.S. Government Printing Office, 1981. GPO stock no. 024-016-00146-0.

Vision, Inc. *Sign Sense: Arlington, Massachusetts.* Arlington, Mass.: Arlington Redevelopment Board, 1977.

Building Site

Aldrich, Harl P., Jr. "Preserving the Foundations of Older Buildings: The Importance of Groundwater Levels." *Technology and Conservation,* Summer 1979.

Conover, Herbert S. *Grounds Maintenance Handbook.* 1953. 3rd ed. New York: McGraw-Hill, 1977.

Curtis, John Obed. *Moving Historic Buildings.* Technical Preservation Services Division, U.S. Department of the Interior. Washington, D.C.: U.S. Government Printing Office, 1979. GPO stock no. 024-016-00109-5.

Favretti, Rudy J., and Joy Putman Favretti. *Landscapes and Gardens for Historic Buildings: A Handbook for Reproducing and Creating Authentic Landscape Settings.* Nashville: American Association for State and Local History, 1978.

Halsted, Byron D., ed. *Barns, Sheds and Outbuildings: Placement, Design and Construction.* 1881. Reprint. Brattleboro, Vt.: Stephen Greene Press, 1977.

Kramer, Jack. *Victorian Gardens: How to Plan, Plant and Enjoy 19th-Century Beauty Today.* New York: Harper and Row, 1981.

Leighton, Ann. *American Gardens in the Eighteenth Century: "For Use or for Delight."* Boston: Houghton Mifflin, 1976.

Scott, Frank J. *Victorian Gardens for Victorian Homes. Part One: Suburban Home Grounds.* 1870. Reprint. Watkins Glen, N.Y.: American Life Foundation, 1982.

Starke, Barry W. *Maymont Park—The Italian Garden, Richmond, Virginia: Using HCRS Grant-in-Aid Funds for Landscape Restoration.* Preservation Case Studies. Technical Preservation Services Division, U.S. Department of the Interior. Washington, D.C.: U.S. Government Printing Office, 1980. GPO stock no. 024-016-00137-1.

Van Ravenswaay, Charles. *A Nineteenth-Century Garden.* New York: Universe Books, 1977.

Structural Systems

Becher, Norman. *The Complete Book of Home Inspection.* New York: McGraw-Hill, 1980.

Brown, Robert Wade. *Residential Foundations: Design, Behavior and Repair.* New York: Van Nostrand Reinhold, 1979.

Carson, Alan, and Robert Dunlop. *Inspecting a House: A Guide for Buyers, Owners and Renovators.* New York: Beaufort Books, 1982.

Civic Trust. "The Armitage Report on Heavy Lorries." London: Her Majesty's Stationery Office, 1980. (Civic Trust: 17 Carlton House Terrace, London SW1Y 5AW, England)

Hoffman, George. *How to Inspect a House.* New York: Delacorte, 1979.

Insall, Donald. *The Care of Old Buildings Today.* London: Architectural Press, Whitney Library of Design, 1972.

Moore, Harry B. *Wood-Inhabiting Insects in Houses: Their Identification, Biology, Prevention and Control.* Washington, D.C.: Forest Service, U.S. Department of Agriculture and U.S. Department of Housing and Urban Development, 1979.

Seaquist, Edgar O., Jr. *Diagnosing and Repairing House Structure Problems.* New York: McGraw-Hill, 1980.

Masonry

Conway, Brian D. "Stucco." Illinois Preservation Series, no. 2. Springfield, Ill.: Division of Historic Sites, Illinois Department of Conservation, 1980.

Gilder, Cornelia Brooke. *Property Owner's Guide to the Maintenance and Repair of Stone Buildings.* Technical Series, no. 5. Albany: Preservation League of New York State, 1977.

Grimmer, Anne E. "Dangers of Abrasive Cleaning to Historic Buildings." Preservation Brief no. 6. Technical Preservation Services Division, U.S. Department of the Interior. Washington, D.C.: U.S. Government Printing Office, 1979. GPO stock no. 024-016-00112-5.

Mack, Robert C., AIA. "The Cleaning and Waterproof Coating of Masonry Buildings." Preservation Brief no. 1. Technical Preservation Services Division, U.S. Department of the Interior. Washington, D.C.: U.S. Government Printing Office, 1975. GPO stock no. 024-016-00650-8.

———. "Repointing Mortar Joints in Historic Brick Buildings." Preservation Brief no. 2. Technical Preservation Services Division, U.S. Department of the Interior. Washington, D.C.: U.S. Government Printing Office, 1976. GPO stock no. 024-016-00148-6.

McKee, Harley J. *Introduction to Early American Masonry: Stone, Brick, Mortar and Plaster.* Washington, D.C.: Preservation Press, 1973.

"Preservation of Historic Adobe Buildings." Preservation Brief no. 5. Technical Preservation Services Division, U.S. Department of the Interior. Washington, D.C.: U.S. Government Printing Office, 1978. GPO stock no. 024-016-00134-6.

Tiller, deTeel Patterson. "The Preservation of Historic Glazed Architectural Terra-Cotta." Preservation Brief no. 7. Technical Preservation Services Division, U.S. Department of the Interior. Washington, D.C.: U.S. Government Printing Office, 1979. GPO stock no. 024-016-00115-0.

Weiss, Norman R. *Exterior Cleaning of Historic Masonry Buildings.* Technical Preservation Services Division, U.S. Department of the Interior. Washington, D.C.: U.S. Government Printing Office, 1979. GPO stock no. 024-016-00123-1.

Wood

Goodall, Harrison, and Renee Friedman. *Log Structures: Preservation and Problem-Solving.* Nashville: American Association for State and Local History, 1980.

Hindle, Brooke, ed. *America's Wooden Age: Aspects of Its Early Technology.* Tarrytown, N.Y.: Sleepy Hollow Press, 1975.

———. *Material Culture of the Wooden Age.* Tarrytown, N.Y.: Sleepy Hollow Press, 1981.

Merrill, William. "Wood Deterioration: Causes, Detection and Prevention." Technical Leaflet Series, no. 77. Nashville: American Association for State and Local History, 1974.

Myers, John H. "Aluminum and Vinyl Sidings on Historic Buildings." Preservation Brief no. 8. Technical Preservation Services Division, U.S. Department of the Interior. Washington, D.C.: U.S. Government Printing Office, 1979. GPO stock no. 024-016-00116-8.

Phillips, Morgan W., and Judith E. Selwyn. *Epoxies for Wood Repairs in Historic Buildings.* Technical Preservation Services Division, U.S. Department of the Interior. Washington, D.C.: U.S. Government Printing Office, 1978. GPO stock no. 024-016-00095-1.

Sheffer, T.C., and A.F. Verrall. *Principles for Protecting Wood Buildings from Decay.* Forest Service Products Laboratory, U.S. Department of Agriculture. Washington, D.C.: U.S. Government Printing Office, 1973.

Ulrey, Harry F. *Carpenters and Builders Library*, vols. I–IV. Indianapolis: Theodore Audel, 1973.

Architectural Metals

Badger, Daniel D. *Badger's Illustrated Catalogue of Cast-Iron Architecture.* Reprint. New York: Dover, 1981.

Gayle, Margot, and Edmund V. Gillon, Jr. *Cast-Iron Architecture in New York: A Photographic Survey.* New York: Dover, 1974.

Gayle, Margot, David W. Look, AIA, and John G. Waite. *Metals in America's Historic Buildings: Uses and Preservation Treatments.* Technical Preservation Services Division, U.S. Department of the Interior. Washington, D.C.: U.S. Government Printing Office, 1980. GPO stock no. 024-016-00143-5.

Organ, Robert M. "The Corrosion of Tin, Copper, Iron and Steel and Lead." In *Preservation and Conservation: Principles and Practices.* Washington, D.C.: Preservation Press, 1976.

Peterson, Harold L. *Conservation of Metals.* Technical Leaflet Series, no. 10. Nashville: American Association for State and Local History, 1968.

Sonn, Albert H. *Early American Wrought Iron.* 1928. Reprint. New York: Bonanza Books, 1979.

Southworth, Susan and Michael. *Ornamental Ironwork: An Illustrated Guide to Its Design, History and Use In American Architecture.* Boston: David R. Godine, 1978.

Wickersham, J.B. *Victorian Ironwork: A Catalogue by J.B. Wickersham.* 1857. Reprint. Introduction by Margot Gayle. Philadelphia: The Athenaeum, 1977.

Roofs and Roofing

Brann, Donald R. *Roofing Simplified.* Rev. ed. Briarcliff Manor, N.Y.: Directions Simplified, 1977.

Bulletin, Association for Preservation Technology, vol. 2, nos. 1–2, 1970.

National Slate Association. *Slate Roofs.* 1926. Rev. reprint. Fairhaven, Vt.: Vermont Structural Slate Company, 1977.

Sweetser, Sarah M. "Roofing for Historic Buildings." Preservation Brief no. 4. Technical Preservation Services Division, U.S. Department of the Interior. Washington, D.C.: U.S. Government Printing Office, 1978. GPO stock no. 024-016-00102-5.

Waite, Diana S. *Nineteenth Century Tin Roofing and Its Use at Hyde Hall.* Albany: New York State Historic Trust, 1971.

———. "Roofing for Early America." In *Building Early America: Contributions Toward the History of a Great Industry.* Edited by Charles E. Peterson. Radnor, Pa.: Chilton Book Company, 1976.

White, Richard. *Olmsted Park System—Jamaica Pond Boathouse, Jamaica Plain, Massachusetts: Planning for Preservation of the Boathouse Roof.* Preservation Case Studies. Technical Preservation Services Division, U.S. Department of the Interior. Washington, D.C.: U.S. Government Printing Office, 1979. GPO stock no. 024-016-00121-4.

Windows and Doors

"Architectural Glass: History and Conservation." *Bulletin*, Association for Preservation Technology, vol. 13, no. 3, 1981.

Eastwood, Maudie. *The Antique Doorknob.* Tillamook, Ore.: Author (3900 Latimer Road North, 97141), 1976.

Myers, John H. "The Repair of Historic Wooden Windows." Preservation Brief no. 9. Technical Preservation Services Division, U.S. Department of the Interior. Washington, D.C.: U.S. Government Printing Office, 1981. GPO stock no. 024-016-00147-8.

Russell and Erwin Manufacturing Company. *Illustrated Catalog of American Hardware of the Russell and Erwin Manufacturing Company: An Unabridged Reprint of the 1865 Edition.* Introduction by Lee H. Nelson. Ottawa: Association for Preservation Technology, 1980.

Shurcliff, William A. *Thermal Shutters and Shades: Over 100 Schemes for Reducing Heat Loss Through Windows.* Andover, Mass.: Brick House Publishing, 1980.

"Special Window Issue." *Old-House Journal,* April 1982.

Wilson, H. Weber. *Your Residential Stained Glass: A Practical Guide to Repair and Maintenance.* Chambersburg, Pa.: Architectural Ecology, 1979.

Wilson, Kenneth M. "Window Glass in America." In *Building Early America: Contributions Toward the History of a Great Industry.* Edited by Charles E. Peterson. Radnor, Pa.: Chilton Book Company, 1976.

Storefronts

Bryan, John M., and Triad Architectural Associates. *Abbeville, South Carolina: Using Grant-in-Aid Funds for Rehabilitation Planning and Project Work in the Commercial Town Square.* Preservation Case Studies. Technical Preservation Services Division, U.S. Department of the Interior, Washington, D.C.: U.S. Government Printing Office, 1979. GPO stock no. 024-016-00126-5.

Cultural Resources Division, Rocky Mountain Regional Office, National Park Service. "The Preservation of Historic Pigmented Structural Glass (Vitrolite and Carrara Glass)." Denver, Colo.: U.S. Department of the Interior, 1981.

Guthrie, Susan. *Main Street Historic District, Van Buren, Arkansas: Using Grant-in-Aid Funds for Storefront Rehabilitation/Restoration Within a Districtwide Plan.* Preservation Case Studies. Technical Preservation Services Division, U.S. Department of the Interior, Washington, D.C.: U.S. Government Printing Office, 1980. GPO stock no. 024-016-00136-2.

Marsh, Ellen. "An Introduction to Storefront Rehabilitation." *Conserve Neighborhoods,* Summer 1979. Washington, D.C.: National Trust for Historic Preservation, 1979.

Mintz, Norman M. "A Practical Guide to Storefront Rehabilitation." Technical Series, no. 2. Albany: Preservation League of New York State, 1977.

Park, Sharon C., AIA. *Storefront Rehabilitation—A 19th Century Commercial Building: The Harding Building, Jackson, Mississippi.* Preservation Case Studies. Technical Preservation Services Division, U.S. Department of the Interior. Washington, D.C.: U.S. Government Printing Office, 1980. GPO stock no. 024-016-00138-9.

Rifkind, Carole. *Main Street: The Face of Urban America.* New York: Harper and Row, 1977.

Entrances, Porches and Steps

Freeman, John Crosby, and Clem Labine. "In Praise of Porches." *Old-House Journal,* August 1981.

Jones, Larry. "Restoring Crumbling Porches." *Old-House Journal,* October 1981.

Micanek, Gary A. "Restoring Porch Latticework." *Old-House Journal,* June 1978.

Phillips, Morgan W. *The Morse-Libby Mansion, Portland, Maine: A Report on Restoration Work, 1973–1977.* Preservation Case Studies. Technical Preservation Services Division, U.S. Department of the Interior. Washington, D.C.: U.S. Government Printing Office, 1977. GPO stock no. 024-005-00699-1.

Exterior Finishes

Batcheler, Penelope Hartshorne. "Paint Color Research and Restoration." Technical Leaflet Series, no. 15. Nashville: American Association for State and Local History, 1968.

Cawley, Frederick D. *Property Owner's Guide to Paint Restoration and Preservation.* Technical Series, no. 1. Albany: Preservation League of New York State, 1976.

Gilbert, Edward R. *Historic House Paint Analysis.* Slide and tape show. Nashville: American Association for State and Local History, 1980.

"How to Assure a Satisfactory Paint Job." Scientific Section, Circular 784. Washington, D.C.: National Paint, Varnish and Lacquer Association, n.d.

Miller, Kevin H., ed. *Paint Color Research and Restoration of Historic Paint.* Ottawa: Association for Preservation Technology, 1977.

Moss, Roger A. *Century of Color: Exterior Decoration for American Buildings, 1820–1920.* Watkins Glen, N.Y.: American Life Foundation, 1980.

National Decorating Products Association. *Paint Problem Solver.* St. Louis: Author, 1980.

National Paint and Coatings Association. *The Household Paint Selector: How to Save Money by Picking the Right Paint for the Right Surface.* New York: Barnes and Noble, 1975.

Pomada, Elizabeth, and Michael Larsen. *Painted Ladies: San Francisco's Resplendent Victorians.* New York: E.P. Dutton, 1978.

Interior Features

Beecher, Catharine E., and Harriet Beecher Stowe. *American Woman's Home.* 1869. Reprint. Introduction and bibliography by Joseph S. Van Why. Watkins Glen, N.Y.: American Life Foundation, 1975.

Blackburn, Graham. *Illustrated Interior Carpentry.* Indianapolis: Bobbs-Merrill, 1978.

Eastlake, Charles L. *Hints on Household Taste in Furniture, Upholstery, and Other Details.* 1878. Reprint. New York: Dover, 1969.

Frangiamore, Catherine Lynn. *Wallpapers in Historic Preservation*. Technical Preservation Services Division, U.S. Department of the Interior. Washington, D.C.: U.S. Government Printing Office, 1977. GPO stock no. 024-005-00685-1.

Garrett, Elisabeth Donaghy, ed. *The Antiques Book of American Interiors: Colonial and Federal Styles*. Main Street Press. New York: Crown, 1980.

———. *The Antiques Book of Victorian Interiors*. Main Street Press. New York: Crown, 1981.

Grow, Lawrence, ed. *The Old-House Book Series: Living Rooms and Parlors; Bedrooms; Kitchens and Dining Rooms; Outdoor Living Spaces*. New York: Warner Books, 1980–81.

Hand, Jackson. *How to Repair, Renovate and Decorate Your Walls, Floors and Ceilings*. New York: Harper and Row, 1976.

Lancaster, Clay. *New York Interiors at the Turn of the Century in 131 Photographs by Joseph Byron from the Byron Collection of the Museum of the City of New York*. New York: Dover, 1976.

Mayhew, Edgar deN., and Minor Myers, Jr. *A Documentary History of American Interiors from the Colonial Era to 1915*. New York: Charles Scribner's Sons, 1980.

Myers, Denys Peter. *Gaslighting in America: A Guide for Historic Preservation*. Technical Preservation Services Division, U.S. Department of the Interior. Washington, D.C.: U.S. Government Printing Office, 1978. GPO stock no. 024-016-00094-3.

Nelson, Lee. "Nail Chronology as an Aid to Dating Old Buildings." Technical Leaflet Series, no. 48. Nashville: American Association for State and Local History, 1968.

Peterson, Harold L. *American Interiors: From Colonial Times to the Late Victorian*. A Pictorial Source Book of American Domestic Interiors with an Appendix on Inns and Taverns. 1971. Reprint. New York: Charles Scribner's Sons, 1979.

Seale, William. *Recreating the Historic House Interior*. Nashville: American Association for State and Local History, 1979.

———. *The Tasteful Interlude: American Interiors Through the Camera's Eye, 1860–1917*. Rev. ed. Nashville: American Association for State and Local History, 1980.

Stickley, Gustav. *Craftsman Homes: Architecture and Furnishings of the American Arts and Crafts Movement*. 1909. Reprint. New York: Dover, 1979.

Wharton, Edith, and Ogden Codman, Jr. *The Decoration of Houses*. 1897. Reprint. Introductions by John Barrington Bayley and William A. Coles. New York: W.W. Norton, 1978.

White, Frank G. *Hardware Restoration*. Slide and tape show. Nashville: American Association for State and Local History, 1977.

New Construction

Armstrong, Richard S., for Cheswick Center. "The Preservation of Churches, Synagogues and Other Religious Structures." Information Series, no. 17. Washington, D.C.: Preservation Press, 1978.

Brolin, Brent C. *Architecture in Context: Fitting New Buildings with Old*. New York: Van Nostrand Reinhold, 1980.

Brown, Floy A. *Chateau Clare, Woonsocket, Rhode Island; Rodman Candleworks, New Bedford, Massachusetts: Rehabilitation Through Federal Assistance*. Preservation Case Studies. Technical Preservation Services Division, U.S. Department of the Interior. Washington, D.C.: U.S. Government Printing Office, 1979. GPO stock no. 024-016-00119-2.

Bunnell, Gene, for Massachusetts Department of Community Affairs. *Built to Last: A Handbook on Recycling Old Buildings*. Washington, D.C.: Preservation Press, 1977.

Cantacuzino, Sherban. *New Uses for Old Buildings*. New York: Whitney Library of Design, 1975.

Cantacuzino, Sherban, and Susan Brandt. *Saving Old Buildings*. London: Architectural Press, 1980.

National Trust for Historic Preservation, ed. *Old and New Architecture: Design Relationship*. Washington, D.C.: Preservation Press, 1980.

———. "Preservation and Recycling of Buildings for Bank Use." Information Series, no. 18. Washington, D.C.: Preservation Press, 1978.

Ray, Keith, ed. *Contextual Architecture: Responding to Existing Style*. New York: Architectural Record Books, McGraw-Hill, 1980.

Schmertz, Mildred F., and Architectural Record Editors. *New Life for Old Buildings*. New York: Architectural Record Books, McGraw-Hill, 1982.

Stoddard, Robert. "Preservation of Concert Halls, Opera Houses and Movie Palaces." Information Series, no. 16. 1978. Rev. ed. Washington, D.C.: Preservation Press, 1981.

Thomas, Margaret A. *Carr Mill, Carrboro, North Carolina: A Rehabilitation Project Under the Tax Reform Act of 1976*. Preservation Case Studies. Technical Preservation Services Division, U.S. Department of the Interior. Washington, D.C.: U.S. Government Printing Office, 1979. GPO stock no. 024-016-00117-6.

Thompson, Elizabeth Kendall, ed. *Recycling Buildings: Renovations, Remodelings, Restorations and Reuses*. New York: Architectural Record Books, McGraw-Hill, 1977.

Urban Land Institute. *Adaptive Use: Development Economics, Process and Profiles*. Washington, D.C.: Author, 1978.

U.S. Department of the Interior and U.S. Department of Housing and Urban Development. *Guidelines for Rehabilitating Old Buildings: Principles to Consider When Planning Rehabilitation and New Construction Projects in Older Neighborhoods*. Washington, D.C.: U.S. Government Printing Office, 1976.

Warner, Raynor M., Sibyl M. Groff and Ranne P. Warner, for Inform, Inc. *New Profits from Old Buildings: Private Enterprise Approaches to Making Preservation Pay*. 1978. Reprint. New York: McGraw-Hill, 1979.

Will, Margaret Thomas. *Recycled Buildings: A Bibliography of Adaptive Use Literature Since 1970*. Monticello, Ill.: Vance Bibliographies, 1979.

Mechanical Systems

American Planning Association, for U.S. Department of Housing and Urban Development with U.S. Department of Energy. *Residential Solar Design Review: A Manual on Community Architectural Controls and Solar Energy Use*. Washington, D.C.: U.S. Government Printing Office, 1980. HUD-PDR-579.

American Society of Heating, Refrigerating and Air Conditioning Engineers. *ASHRAE Handbook and Product Directory: 1977 Fundamentals*. New York: Author, 1977.

Chambers, J. Henry, AIA. *Cyclical Maintenance for Historic Buildings*. Technical Preservation Services Division, U.S. Department of the Interior. Washington, D.C.: U.S. Government Printing Office, 1979. GPO stock no. 024-005-00637-1.

Mazria, Edward. *The Passive Solar Energy Book: A Complete Guide to Passive Solar Home, Greenhouse and Building Design*. Emmaus, Pa.: Rodale Press, 1979.

National Trust for Historic Preservation, ed. *New Energy from Old Buildings*. Washington, D.C.: Preservation Press, 1981.

Reif, Daniel K. *Solar Retrofit: Adding Solar to Your Home*. Andover, Mass.: Brick House Publishing, 1981.

Smith, Baird M., AIA. "Conserving Energy in Historic Buildings." Preservation Brief no. 3. Technical Preservation Services Division, U.S. Department of the Interior. Washington, D.C.: U.S. Government Printing Office, 1976. GPO stock no. 024-016-00103-6.

Vonier, Thomas, AIA, and Peter H. Smeallie, for Technical Preservation Services Division, U.S. Department of the Interior. *Energy Conservation and Solar Energy from Historic Buildings: Guidelines for Appropriate Designs*. Washington, D.C.: National Center for Architecture and Urbanism, 1981.

Wing, Charles. *From the Walls In*. Boston: Atlantic Monthly Press, Little, Brown, 1979.

Safety and Code Requirements

American National Standards Institute. *Specifications for Making Buildings and Facilities Accessible to and Usable by Physically Handicapped People*. ANSI A117.1 (1980). New York: Author, 1980.

Architectural and Transportation Barriers Compliance Board. *A Guidebook to the Minimum Federal Guidelines and Requirements for Accessible Design*. Washington, D.C.: National Conference of States on Building Codes and Standards, 1981.

Botsai, Elmer E., FAIA, et al. *Architects and Earthquakes*. Division of Advanced Environmental Research and Technology, Research Applications, National Science Foundation. Washington, D.C.: U.S. Government Printing Office, 1978. GPO stock no. 038-000-00331-3.

Green, Melvyn, and Harriet Watson. *Alternative Life Safety Systems for Historic Structures*. El Sugundo, Calif.: Author (690 N. Sepulveda Boulevard, no. 120, 90245), 1976.

Kenney, Alice P. *Access to the Past: Museum Progams and Handicapped Visitors*. Nashville: American Association for State and Local History, 1980.

Keune, Russell V., AIA, for National Trust for Historic Preservation. *Assessment of Current Building Regulatory Methods as Applied to the Needs of Historic Preservation Projects*. National Bureau of Standards, Special Publication no. 524, U.S. Department of Commerce. Washington, D.C.: U.S. Government Printing Office, 1978. GPO stock no. 003-003-01990-9.

McCartney, Henry, and Maureen F. Pepson, with The Conservancy Group. "Stop Arson." *Conserve Neighborhoods*, January-February 1982. National Trust for Historic Preservation.

Milner, Margaret. *Adapting Historic Campus Structures for Accessibility*. Washington, D.C.: Association for Physical Plant Administrators of Universities and Colleges and National Center for a Barrier Free Environment, 1980.

National Institute of Building Sciences. *Rehabilitation Guidelines*. U.S. Department of Housing and Urban Development. Washington, D.C.: U.S. Government Printing Office, 1980.

Parrott, Charles. *Access to Historic Buildings for the Disabled: Suggestions for Planning and Implementation*. Technical Preservation Services Division, U.S. Department of the Interior. Washington, D.C.: U.S. Government Printing Office, 1980. GPO stock no. 024-016-00149-4.

"Regulating Existing Buildings." *Bulletin*, Association for Preservation Technology, vol. 13, no. 2, 1981.

Vitale, Edmund. *Building Regulations: A Self-Help Guide for the Owner-Builder*. New York: Charles Scribner's Sons, 1979.

Weisman, Herman M., ed. *Arson Resource Directory*. 2nd ed. Washington, D.C.: Arson Resource Center, Federal Emergency Management Agency, 1981.

Technical Preservation Services
Preservation Assistance Division
National Park Service
U.S. Department of the Interior
Washington, D.C. 20240

Sets technical preservation standards and guidelines for work undertaken on historic buildings; provides to the regions technical preservation policy guidance for tax incentive rehabilitation certifications; develops technical preservation information for federal agencies, state and local governments and individuals; and reports annually to Congress on endangered National Historic Landmarks.

National Trust for Historic Preservation
1785 Massachusetts Avenue, N.W.
Washington, D.C. 20036

As the leading national private preservation organization, coordinates efforts of preservation groups, provides professional advice, conducts conferences, administers financial aid programs, issues publications and maintains historic properties. Membership is open to all interested people and organizations. Advisory services also are provided from six regional offices:

Northeast Regional Office
Old City Hall
45 School Street
Boston, Mass. 02110

Mid-Atlantic Regional Office
1600 H Street, N.W.
Washington, D.C. 20006

Southern Regional Office
456 King Street
Charleston, S.C. 29403

Midwest Regional Office
407 South Dearborn, Suite 710
Chicago, Ill. 60605

Mountains/Plains Regional Office
1407 Larimer Street, Suite 200
Denver, Colo. 80202

Western Regional Office
681 Market Street, Suite 859
San Francisco, Calif. 94105

American Association for State and Local History
708 Berry Road
Nashville, Tenn. 37204

Serves historical societies and professional and amateur historians through extensive publications, such as books and technical leaflets on rehabilitation, as well as through training programs.

Association for Preservation Technology
P.O. Box 2487, Station D
Ottawa, Ontario KIP 5W6, Canada

An organization of professional preservationists and conservators that promotes preservation research and provides technical information through publications and workshops.

The Victorian Society in America
The Athenaeum
East Washington Square
Philadelphia, Pa. 19106

Promotes the preservation of Victorian-era buildings and culture through publications, local chapters, conferences and tours.

Society for the Preservation of New England Antiquities
141 Cambridge Street
Boston, Mass. 02114

Provides advisory services to owners of historic properties as an outgrowth of conservation work on its own properties.

National Register of Historic Places
Interagency Resources Management Division
National Park Service
U.S. Department of the Interior
Washington, D.C. 20240

Maintains the official inventory of buildings, districts, sites, structures and objects determined to be worthy of preservation because of their significance in American history, architecture, archeology and culture. The office provides information on how to obtain National Register listing.

State Historic Preservation Offices

Agencies in each state and U.S. territory designated to administer public state preservation programs, including cultural resource surveys and inventories, preparation of statewide preservation plans, processing of nominations to the National Register of Historic Places, maintenance of state landmarks registers and related preservation activities. A list of state historic preservation offices is available from the National Conference of State Historic Preservation Officers, 1522 K Street, N.W., Washington, D.C. 20005.

Other Sources of Information

Advisory Council on Historic Preservation
1522 K Street, N.W., Suite 530
Washington, D.C. 20005

Alliance for Historic Landscape Preservation
P.O. Box 3243, Station C
Ottawa, Ontario KIY 4J5, Canada

American Institute of Architects
Committee on Historic Resources
1735 New York Avenue, N.W.
Washington, D.C. 20006

American Society of Interior Designers
Historic Preservation and Adaptive Reuse Committee
730 Fifth Avenue
New York, N.Y. 10019

American Society of Landscape Architects
Committee on Historic Preservation
1733 Connecticut Avenue, N.W.
Washington, D.C. 20009

Friends of Cast-Iron Architecture
235 East 87th Street, Room 6C
New York, N.Y. 10028

Friends of Terra Cotta
c/o California Historical Society
2090 Jackson Street
San Francisco, Calif. 94109

Garden Clubs of America
Conservation Committee
598 Madison Avenue
New York, N.Y. 10022

Historic House Association of America
1600 H Street, N.W.
Washington, D.C. 20006

Society for Commercial Archeology
c/o Museum of Transportation
300 Congress Street
Boston, Mass. 02210

Society for Industrial Archeology
c/o National Museum of American History
Room 5020
Smithsonian Institution
Washington, D.C. 20560

Society of Architectural Historians
1700 Walnut Street, Suite 716
Philadelphia, Pa. 19103

PHOTOGRAPH CREDITS

Getting Started

A Middletown, Conn., house before rehabilitation. Photograph by Carleton Knight III, National Trust for Historic Preservation.

The Environment

Howe Farms in Tunbridge, Vt. Photograph courtesy Vermont Travel Division.

Building Site

The pergola in the Pioneer Square Historic District, Seattle, Wash. Photograph by Carleton Knight III, National Trust for Historic Preservation.

Structural Systems

Exposed dome of the Baltimore City Hall (1867–75, George A. Frederick) during restoration. Photograph by Charles L. Hammond, Jr.

Masonry

Old U.S. Post Office (1891–99, Willoughby J. Edbrooke), Washington, D.C. Photograph by Baird M. Smith, AIA.

Wood

Amariah T. Prouty House (c. 1853), Kalamazoo, Mich. Photograph by Balthazar Korab.

Architectural Metals

Cast-iron fronts of commercial buildings (1866) on East Main Street, Richmond, Va. Photograph by Robert Winthrop.

Roofs and Roofing

Lower Pontalba Building (1849–51) on Jackson Square, New Orleans. Photograph by Mary Oehrlein, Building Conservation Technology, Inc.

Windows and Doors

Columbia Congregational Church (1832), Columbia, Conn. Photograph © Philip Trager 1977.

Storefronts

Late 19th-century storefront, Madison, Ind. Photograph by James L. Ballard, National Trust for Historic Preservation.

Entrances, Porches and Steps

House (c. 1890) on Litchfield Avenue, Torrington, Conn. Photograph © Philip Trager 1977.

Exterior Finishes

Carson House (1884–86, Samuel and Joseph C. Newsom), Eureka, Calif. Photograph from Library of Congress collection.

Interior Features

Grand Concourse Restaurant, Pittsburgh and Lake Erie Terminal Building (1898–1901, William George Burns), Pittsburgh, Pa. Photograph courtesy Pittsburgh History and Landmarks Foundation.

New Construction

Trentman House (1968, Hugh Newell Jacobsen), Georgetown, Washington, D.C. Photograph by Robert C. Lautman.

Mechanical Systems

Furnace at Olana (1874, Calvert Vaux), Church Hill, N.Y. Photograph by Cervin Robinson, Historic American Buildings Survey.

Safety and Code Requirements

Ramp for handicapped at National Trust for Historic Preservation headquarters (1915–17, Jules Henri de Sibour), Washington, D.C. Photograph by Walter Smalling, Jr.

Standards and Guidelines

Rehabilitated row houses on 17th Avenue, Portland, Ore. Photograph by Ed Hershberger.

Other Books from
THE PRESERVATION PRESS

American Landmarks: Properties of the National Trust for Historic Preservation. Features the 13 National Trust museum properties, from an 18th-century Virginia house associated with Jefferson to 20th-century innovations by Frank Lloyd Wright. The descriptions detail the construction, style, occupants, furnishings, preservation and interpretation by the Trust. 72 pages, illustrated. $5.95 paperbound.

America's Forgotten Architecture. National Trust for Historic Preservation, Tony P. Wrenn, Elizabeth D. Mulloy. The best overview of preservation today, the book surveys in 475 photographs what is worth saving and how to do it. 312 pages, illustrated, bibliography, appendixes. Published by Pantheon Books. $20 clothbound, $12.95 paperbound.

Economic Benefits of Preserving Old Buildings. Shows how recycling buildings for new uses saves money. Examples of projects—large and small, public and private—are provided along with construction and financial details. 168 pages, illustrated. $7.95 paperbound.

Fabrics for Historic Buildings. Jane C. Nylander. 2nd edition. A popular guide that gives practical advice on selecting and using reproductions of historic fabrics. A key feature is an illustrated catalog listing 300 reproduction fabrics. Also included are a glossary and list of manufacturers. 68 pages, illustrated, glossary, bibliography. $6.95 paperbound.

"I Feel I Should Warn You . . ." Historic Preservation Cartoons. Terry B. Morton, ed. Essay by Draper Hill. A unique collection of cartoons that have nipped and nudged to keep the wreckers at bay for more than 150 years. The book also highlights some renowned preservation wins and losses. 113 pages, illustrated. $5.95 paperbound, $8.95 clothbound.

Information: A Preservation Sourcebook. A compendium of two dozen publications from the National Trust "Information" series. Topics range from basic preservation procedures and rehabilitation of old houses to public and private financing, revolving funds, economic benefits of preservation and special building types. Annually updated for permanent reference. 600 pages, illustrated, bibliography. $25 binder. Supplements, $5 each.

Introduction to Early American Masonry: Stone, Brick, Mortar and Plaster. Harley J. McKee, FAIA. Classic guide to masonry construction and conservation that examines the origins, use, manufacture, styles, deterioration and restoration of each masonry type. 92 pages, illustrated, bibliography, index. $6.95 paperbound.

New Energy from Old Buildings. Details the energy conservation benefits of recycling old buildings and describes how to safeguard them during retrofitting for conservation and solar applications. 208 pages, illustrated, glossary, bibliography, index. $9.95 paperbound.

Presence of the Past: A History of the Preservation Movement in the U.S. Before Williamsburg. Charles B. Hosmer, Jr. A thorough and entertaining account of early preservationists and their landmark achievements. Famous battles to save such sites as Mount Vernon and Monticello are recounted along with the personalities of the first American preservationists. 386 pages, illustrated, bibliography, index. $12.95 clothbound.

Preservation Comes of Age: From Williamsburg to the National Trust, 1926–1949. Charles B. Hosmer, Jr. The second volume in the author's monumental history of preservation documents the period when preservation became a national policy. Its coverage ranges from the birth of local historic districts through innovative federal programs of the 1930s and 1940s to the founding of the National Trust. Key campaigns, people and preservation principles are highlighted throughout. Published by the University Press of Virginia. 1,291 pages, illustrated, bibliography, chronology, index. $37.50 clothbound (2 vols.).

Preservation and Conservation: Principles and Practices. An in-depth examination of the technical aspects of restoration and object conservation, from preservation philosophy and education to restoration materials, techniques and maintenance, with case studies. 547 pages, illustrated, bibliography. $17.95 paperbound.

What Style Is It? John Poppeliers, S. Allen Chambers, Nancy B. Schwartz. One of the most popular concise guides to American architectural styles, prepared by staff of the Historic American Buildings Survey. 48 pages, illustrated, glossary, bibliography. $4.95 paperbound.

To order Preservation Press books, send total of book prices (less 10 percent discount for National Trust members), plus $2.50 postage and handling, to: Preservation Bookshop, 1600 H Street, N.W., Washington, D.C. 20006. Residents of California, the District of Columbia, Massachusetts, New York and South Carolina please add applicable sales tax. Make checks payable to the National Trust and allow at least three weeks for delivery.

A complete list of publications is available by writing: The Preservation Press, National Trust for Historic Preservation, 1785 Massachusetts Avenue, N.W., Washington, D.C. 20036.